1

Secrets
of the Ninja

Secrets
of the Ninja

Ashida Kim

Paladin Press
Boulder, Colorado

Secrets of the Ninja
by Ashida Kim
Copyright © 1981 by Ashida Kim

ISBN 0-87364-234-1
Printed in the United States of America

Published by Paladin Press, a division of
Paladin Enterprises, Inc., P.O. Box 1307,
Boulder, Colorado 80306, USA.
(303) 443-7250

Direct inquiries and/or orders to the above address.

To Kojin Sha,
whose shadow
still lives

Contents

Preface

Secrets of the Ninja is intended purely as a study of an ancient and obscure martial arts form. It is designed to provide a complete overview of Ninjitsu. Facets of this rarest of all martial forms covered in the following pages include meditation, mind clouding, entering and escaping, sentry removal, weapons, climbing, and other related considerations. Most often the scenario entails a Ninja entering an armed camp for the purposes of committing espionage, sabotage, and/or assassination.

The principles and forms presented herein are oriented toward use by a lone individual. Some *ryu* (schools) advocate the use of such equipment as shuriken, grapples, shaken, and even poisons and firearms. These schools train to use or improvise any weapon that may further aid the mission. Indeed, the Ninja was once expected to be a weapons master. There is much to be said about this approach to Ninjitsu; this overview, therefore, includes sections explaining the classical Ninja use of several weapons.

Yet study of the art as a whole does not require weapons of any type. Sensei once said that "a naked man, alone, in an empty room, can practice Ninjitsu." One cannot move quickly and silently when encumbered by various tools, and if captured, they would certainly be confiscated. What is one to do then?

Here are the means to be invisible in the presence of the enemy, to penetrate unseen anywhere, and to pass without leaving a trace.

This is the Way of Ninjitsu, the Art of Invisibility.

ON ESPIONAGE AS A WEAPON

About five hundred years before the birth of Christ, a Chinese philosopher named Sun-tse stated in his "Rules for Political and Psychological Subversion" that "there is no art higher than that of destroying the enemy's resistance without a fight on the battlefield. According to the philosopher,

> The direct tactic of war is necessary only on the battlefield, but only the indirect tactic can lead to a real and lasting victory.
>
> Subvert anything of value in the enemy's country. Implicate the emissaries of the major powers in criminal undertakings; undermine their position and destroy their reputation in other ways as well; and expose them to the public ridicule of their fellow citizens.
>
> Do not shun the aid of even the lowest and the most despicable people. Disrupt the work of their government with every means you can.
>
> Spread disunity and dispute among the citizens of the enemy's country. Turn the young against the old. Use every means to destroy their arms, their supplies, and the discipline of the enemy's forces.
>
> Debase old traditions and accepted gods. Be generous with promises and rewards to purchase intelligence and accomplices. Send out your secret agents in all directions. Do not skimp with money or with promises, for they yield a high return.

It is upon this passage from *The Art of War* that Ninjitsu is based. Sun-tse was correct. No more need be said concerning espionage as a weapon.

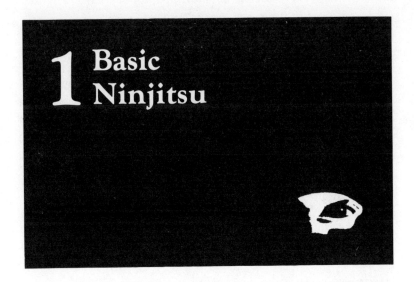

1 Basic Ninjitsu

The origins of Ninjitsu are shrouded in the mists of time. It was greatly influenced by Chinese spying techniques, many of which are found in Sun-tse's classic, *The Art of War*. The word *Ninjitsu* itself originated during a war between Prince Shotoku and Moriya over the land of Omi in sixth century Japan. During this conflict a warrior named Otomo-no-Saajin contributed to the victory of Prince Shotoku by secretly gathering valuable intelligence about the enemy forces. For this service, he was awarded the title of *Shinobi*, which means "stealer-in." From this ideogram the character for *Ninjitsu* is derived.

Originally, the role of a Ninja was to gain information about the enemy and to sabotage his operations. Agents were classified as: *indigenous,* meaning natives who gathered intelligence; *inside,* an agent within the enemy establishment; *sleeper,* being one who is in position awaiting the order to act; *doubled,* a former agent of the enemy who spied for both sides; and *expendable* agents who were used for one mission. Agents included both men and women; the female Ninja was called *kunoichi* and carried out missions of assassination and sabotage, as well as espionage.

Ninjitsu is *not* a magical technique which will enable you to disassemble your body and reassemble yourself somewhere else. It will not change the structure of your body, making it transparent. This art of invisibility consists of the skills you employ to make yourself unseeable; in this context, the art becomes almost a philosophy.

The ancient masters have said, "A tree falling in the forest with no one to hear, makes no sound; but it falls nonetheless." So it is with

1

Ninjitsu. A Ninja attacking a blind man is invisible, but he is attacking nonetheless.

TO BE A NINJA

To be a Ninja, indeed even to contemplate the Silent Way, one must be a hunter. This means that he knows the ways of his prey. He studies their habits, patterns of movement, and routines. In this way, he can strike when they are most vulnerable, or trap them in their own habits.

To be a Ninja, an invisible assassin, one must be a warrior. This means that he accepts responsibility for his actions. Strategy is the craft of the warrior.

To be a Ninja, one must be a wizard. This means that he can "stop the world" and see with the "eyes of God." This is the essence of *Mugei-Mumei No-Jitsu,* which is translated to mean, "no name, no art."

UNIFORM OF THE NINJA

The costume of the Ninja is basically that of the stage handlers of the kabuki theater, who sneak on stage during scenes to help actors with costume changes, move scenery, or remove props. He is not noticed, even though he may remain in full view for an entire act; he seems a part of the landscape, and when he does move it is accomplished so swiftly and unobtrusively that he escapes notice.

For our purpose, the Ninja uniform will consist of: (*a*) black ski mask, as camouflage paint or "blacking" the face is time consuming and cannot be quickly removed; (*b*) black overjacket; (*c*) black belt or sash; (*d*) black coveralls, with blousing ties at the wrists and ankles; and (*e*) black tabi, split-toed socks made for wearing with sandals— the soft sole of these protects the feet and helps to muffle sounds of walking. The traditional uniform included the *hakima* which is a divided skirt for formal wear, leggings, and a light tunic of chain mail. Sensei also employed a large, hooded cape, which was used to distort the silhouette.

PRINCIPLES OF LIGHT AND SHADOW

Since any opaque object absorbs light, it produces a shadow in the space behind it. If the source of light is a point, an opaque surface cuts off all light striking it, producing a shadow of uniform density. An example is the casting of hand shadows on a wall.

If the source of light is larger than a point, the shadow varies in intensity, creating the *umbra* and *penumbra*. The former is that portion from which all rays of light are obscured, while the penumbra is the lighter part, not entirely hidden from the observer.

Spotlights, hand torches, and so on, are points of light. The latter of the two shadows is the more frequently encountered. Thus, in Ninjitsu, we strive to remain in the deepest shadow, the umbra, as this offers the best concealment.

The rule of *kagashi-no-jitsu* states that the eye sees *movement* first, *silhouette* second, and *color* third. Dark adaptation means allowing the eyes to become accustomed to low levels of light. Approximately thirty minutes are required for the rod cells to produce sufficient visual purple to enable the eye to distinguish objects in dim light. Off-center vision is a technique of focusing attention on an object without looking directly at it. When an object is looked at directly, the image is formed on the cone region of the eye. This area is not sensitive at night. When the eye looks five to ten degrees above, below, right, or left of the object, the image falls on the rod cells.

Scanning is a method of using this off-center vision to observe an object or area. During night observation, the visual purple of the rod cells bleaches out in five to ten seconds and the image fades. As this occurs, you must shift the eyes slightly so that fresh rod cells are used. Move the eyes in short irregular intervals over the object, but do not look directly at it. Pause a few seconds at each point of observation because your eyes normally are used where there is sufficient light to create sharp outlines and bright colors. In darkness, objects are faint, have no distinct outline, and little or no color. To move in darkness, you must believe what you see. Only practice can achieve this.

At night, if the enemy can be seen, keep the fire (light) between the two of you. Remember, the enemy is looking from an area of light (in which his pupils have constricted) into an area of darkness, where insufficient light exists to display an image on the cone region of the eye. In daylight, keep the fire and the door on your right, and keep the left side clear.

Moving in the shadows requires that a path be selected from one place of concealment to another, crossing any exposed areas quickly and quietly. Standing in darkness requires great patience and controlled breathing. The best place inside a room is the nearest corner behind the door. Select a shadow to be used and advance silently to it. Assume a posture which conforms to the shape of the shadow and remain within it. Practice shallow breathing.

To become invisible, Ninjitsu employs the Nine Steps of Kuji Ashi. This is consistent with the concept of *Shugendo,* the mountain asceticism of feudal Japan, in which *Kuji* (nine) is the most important number.

2 Meditation For Inner Strength

The emphasis on meditation to cultivate the mind and the body is characteristic of all the Far Eastern martial arts. Nowhere is this more true than in Ninjitsu, the Silent Way.

Ninja place as much importance on the spiritual and mental aspects of their art as on the physical. To this end they have developed exercises to sharpen their perception and psychological insight. These techniques also serve to rejuvenate the body, calm the mind, and cultivate the inner strength. It was said that the ancient Ninja could sense hidden enemies, foresee the imminent death of a sick or aged person, and predict the breakup of a marriage.

STRENGTH—INNER AND OUTER

There are two kinds of strength, just as there are Yin and Yang. The outer, physical strength fades with age and is dissipated by excess; the inner flows through, and with, and from all things. The inner strength is by far the more powerful of the two, but it must be developed through constant practice and study. The *Chi* is a force within all people that can be forged to perform the will. But not one in ten thousand will ever know the true Chi. This cannot be explained, but it can be experienced. The practice is known as *Kuji Kiri.*

The secret of meditation is regular practice. Perseverance, diligence, and quiet determination are required. If performed on a daily basis, continuous improvement may be expected. Meditation is not a process to be hurried; do not expect instant success.

5

Two periods per day are recommended, one soon after rising and one before going to bed. The exercise should be done in a quiet darkened room, neither too warm nor too cold. The clothing should be comfortable, there should be adequate ventilation to provide fresh air; noises or other distractions should be avoided.

Breath control is the key to proper meditation, which may be defined as *the art of consciously altering the state of mind.* To accomplish this, one physically adjusts the pH (acid/alkaline balance) of the blood.

There are drawbacks to this training, however. First, it should not be undertaken by people with heart trouble of any kind. Persons with chronic ailments, diabetes, or similar infirmities should also abstain.

Second, it should not be practiced while under the influence of any form of medication, narcotic, or alcohol. This includes tobacco.

Third, this training is not for the purpose of gaining, exploiting, or manipulating power; Kuji Kiri should not be practiced with those goals in mind.

PHYSICAL PREPARATION

One cannot embark on the path to enlightenment all at once. The body must be prepared. The exercises given here are strenuous in the extreme—some may produce unconsciousness. The shock to the body could be quite severe unless proper precautions are taken.

The following exercises are recommended. They are certainly Chinese in origin, and are an essential part of the Kuji Kiri (nine keys) practice. Likewise, the nine keys form a portion of the larger art of Hsi Men Jitsu, the Way of the Mind Gate.

FIG. 1—Sit in the Lotus position, relax the shoulders, straighten the back, do not lean. Close the eyes and empty the mind. This is sometimes difficult because the mind is full of many things. Try to diminish your thoughts. This will help you see yourself inside. Clench the fists and place them on the thighs palms uppermost. This will aid in clearing thoughts from the mind and enable you to concentrate on the experience of inner energy. Click the teeth together thirty-six times. Do this lightly at an even pace. This calms the heart.

FIG. 2—Interlock the fingers, place the palms on the back of the head, covering the ears. The fingers should touch the base of the skull. Place the thumbs below the ears. Gently apply pressure with the palms, relax the shoulders. This will warm the ears and benefit the kidneys. If your mind is calm, you will feel the beat of your pulse. Breathe gently and slowly without sound nine times. Think of each breath as water filling a glass. The air is drawn into the lower lungs first and fills them from below. When exhaling, let the air flow out of the upper lungs first.

FIG. 1

FIG. 2

Allow the energy of this action to fall to the seat of breathing, the *Hara*. This is the body's physical and spiritual center, located approximately two inches below the navel. You will know when you feel it. The hands continue to rest on the back of the head. Beat the index fingers against the base of the skull at ear level alternately twenty-four times. This will stimulate the brain, prevent deafness, and help one to achieve longevity.

FIG. 3—Open the hands and place them on the thighs. Open the eyes; turn the upper body from the waist, twisting to the left and then to the right forty-eight times. This stimulates and exercises the neck and upper spinal cord.

FIG. 4—Place the left palm over the right and rub them together in a circular manner from left to right twenty-four times. Then reverse the hands, right over left, and repeat. This will stimulate circulation.

The hands are now warm. Place the palms on the back above the kidneys. Rotate both hands vigorously on the back twenty-four times; then hold the hands over the kidneys for a few minutes. This will strengthen the kidneys, improve the posture, and increase vitality. This area is known as the Gate of Life.

Relax, rest the hands on the thighs, close the eyes. You are now ready to begin the breathing exercises.

BREATHING EXERCISES

That a direct relation exists between the breath and the heart rates must be obvious. The following practices are known collectively as Chi Kung—*Chi* meaning breath, and *Kung* meaning pause. Literally, *Chi Kung* translates as *a cessation or pause in the movement of the breath*. This is accomplished in three ways: by *hypoventilation* (holding the breath); by *hyperventilation* (oxygen saturation); or by *proper breathing*.

Hypoventilation makes the blood more acidic by diminishing the amount of oxygen in the blood. It is characterized by a sensation of heat which floods over the body. This also causes the heart to beat faster as it strives to restore the proper pH balance by circulating the blood more quickly.

Hyperventilation is characterized by a chill feeling of cold which permeates the body. It causes the blood to become more alkaline by saturating the system with large amounts of oxygen. This makes the heartbeat slower.

Proper breathing produces a sensation of calmness and relaxation.

FIG. 3

FIG. 4

HYPNOTIC HAND MOVEMENTS

Kuji Kiri is the technique of performing hypnotic movements with the hands. These magical *in-signs* created by knitting the fingers together may be used to restore one's confidence in moments of stress, or to hypnotize an adversary into inaction or temporary paralysis. Each is a key or psychological trigger to a specific center of power in the body. There are three basic positions, corresponding to the three basic Chi Kung techniques. Each of these yields three variations for a total of nine, one for each center. From each of these are derived three variations for each of the three types of energy (Yin, Yang, Tao). These are keyed to the twelve meridians of acupuncture, the four seas of the body, and so on, making a grand total of eighty-one.

CHU (FIRST KANJI)

There are nine basically significant centers of power. The first of these is located at the base of the spine. It controls elimination and corresponds to the sacral plexus. This is the occult center of the body, which holds the serpent power. It also represents the earth element. Its color is yellow. The *Tu Mo,* or Channel of Control, is composed of twenty-eight acupuncture points, ascending from the coccyx, up the spine, over the skull, and ending at the upper gum. If this channel is not functioning properly, one will experience bladder problems, pain in the lower abdomen or chest, or hernia. Many of the points on this channel are employed to stimulate or tone the organs in general. Meditation on this center steadies the body and trains the mind.

FIG. 5—Place the palms facing, thumbs together, fingers upward. Interlock the fingers above, but extend the index fingers of both hands so that they lie side by side. Lift the hands and hold them in front of the chest. Feel the heat between your hands; feel the beat of your pulse in the palms.

FIG. 6—Using the index fingers as a pointer, trace the ideogram shown in the air before you by alternately tracing five horizontal lines and four vertical. Close the eyes and visualize the character. This will key the mind to the sacral center.

Hold the head erect, place the tip of the tongue lightly on the roof of the mouth. Inhale deeply through the nose, filling the lungs from bottom to top. Lay the hands in the lap. Exhale, emptying the lungs from top to bottom, but exhale only two-thirds of the breath. Press the remaining one-third downward into the Hara region. Repeat this breathing exercise eighty-one times.

On the eighty-first exhalation, hold the breath. Think of the Hara—"If this region is warm," say the Chinese, "one is halfway to immor-

FIG. 5

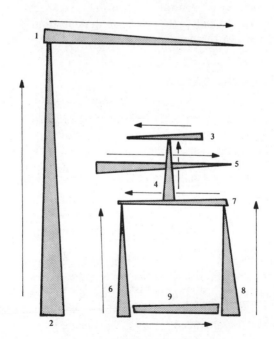

FIG. 6

tality." This exercise alone will prevent many illnesses. Lower the head forward until the chin touches the chest if possible, but do not stretch. This will aid in retaining the breath. *Do not hold the breath with the throat.* This can cause rupturing of the blood vessels supplying the face, neck, and head. Retain the breath by tensing the diaphragm, the bellows which draw the air in and press it downward.

While in this position, one develops a kinesthetic sense of the body. This enables one to diagnose imbalances of energy within the body. The technique is known as *touring.* Holding the breath for 81 heartbeats is known as the Small Tour, in which the grosser aspects of the health are examined. Holding the breath for 108 heartbeats is known as the Grand Tour.

After the prescribed time (number of heartbeats), relax; slowly release the diaphragm taking care not to strain. Release the tension in the Hara, also slowly, taking care not to gulp air and induce belching. The Hara will now feel warm, like a friendly fire. You will feel a sensation stirring at the base of the spine. It will grow, double, redouble, and race up the spine to the base of the skull. This is the site of the medulla oblongata, which controls all of the autonomic reflexes of the body—including respiration, circulation, and certain other functions—hence the Channel of Control. Once in this state, begin sensory withdrawal exercises to isolate the mind and develop conscious control of the body. In yoga the *bandhis,* or muscle locks, are practiced at this stage.

SHEN (SECOND KANJI)

The second center of power is the source of the *Jen Mo,* or Channel of Function. It begins at the base of the genitals and travels up the center of the body, ending on the face just above the chin. Along this path lie twenty-four acupuncture points, or points of adjustment. If there is an imbalance in this channel's flow of energy, the back of the neck will be stiff and there will be spiritual unrest. This center represents the water element. Its form is circular and its color is white. It controls sexual desires and is characterized by the energy of youth. It corresponds to the epigastric plexus and develops power generation in the psychic centers.

FIG. 7—Place the palms together as before and extend the index fingers. Withdraw the middle finger from its intertwined position and place it over the index fingers. Think of the Hara, the One Point.

FIG. 8—Lift the hands and trace the illustrated ideogram in the air before you by alternately tracing five horizontal and four vertical lines. Close the eyes and visualize the character. Place the hands in the lap.

FIG. 7

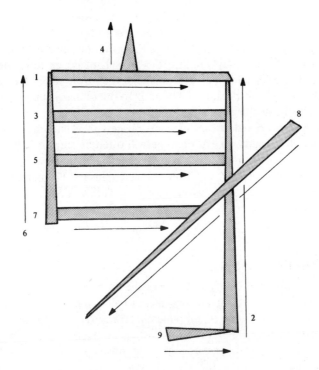

FIG. 8

Hold the head erect. Begin with an exhalation brought about by a rapid inward stroke of the abdomen. Inhalation follows immediately by relaxation of the abdominal muscles. Thus, inhalation is so passive and automatic that one again creates an oxygen debt within the system; as before, this produces a sensation of warmth. Repeat this exercise eighty-one times at the rate of two exhalations per second. Lay the head back, exposing the throat.

On the eighty-first repetition, hold the breath as before with the diaphragm. Previously it was specified that the Lotus posture of yoga be employed for these exercises. The reason will now become apparent. When the breathing exercise described herein is properly performed over a long period, certain vibrations begin within the body. These emanate from the center of power we are now considering. The vibrations, coupled with a feeling of exhilaration, lessen motor control of the limbs. In the Lotus, the legs are in a position impossible to undo without the aid of the hands. Thus they are not likely to be disturbed by this loss of control. Such an occurrence would likely cause one to fall over.

This exercise is used to develop concentration. In the stage of sensory withdrawal, one becomes responsive to those forces which are of a spiritual nature. When the Ninja finds that he can detach himself from senses, he is ready for this, the second, phase. In this state, let the mind wander and your thoughts take their own course freely. At first this is difficult because the mind is so full of many things. After a time, it settles and begins to flow.

This unrestricted stream of consciousness may entertain good as well as evil thoughts, so evil that one will often be surprised. But, day by day, these will diminish, become less and less numerous, and less extensive. Until, finally, only one thought remains. Then attention is directed to the interval between thoughts. The latter are elusive and fluctuating continuously. The former, the interval, is calm and flowing. By this experience one comes to know the true self. This exercise is often taught as a purification ritual.

KAI (THIRD KANJI)

The Hara (One Point) is the site of the third center of power in the body, located approximately two inches below the navel. This is the body's center of gravity. It also represents the water element. From this point flows the *Yang Wei Mo,* or Positive Arm Channel, which rises across the chest and extends down the inner arms to the palm and middle finger tips; and the *Yin Wei Mo,* or Negative Arm Channel, which also passes through the arms, but with the emphasis on veins instead of arteries. If the former (Yang Yu) is affected, the heart will be aggravated, the palms will be feverish, and the arm joints will be stiff. Headaches, fevers, and toothaches are also indicated. If the latter is not functioning properly, nervous disorders, hypertension, and epilepsy may result.

Before the student can begin to practice the actual techniques of Kuji Kiri, he must learn to keep the One Point. By relaxing and concentrating the mind on this, even when moving about in daily life, one is able to achieve perfect balance and mental stability. This develops coordination of mind and body. The next objective is to transmit this power effectively. This involves the concept of Chi, the inner force. Chi is the spirit of the mind. Kuji Kiri teaches us to use it at will. *You must control the One Point to be successful.* In this way, the force will flow as needed.

Control of this center develops the faculty of intuition, increases the power to know oneness, and leads to an understanding of good and evil. Thus it has long been taught by many ryu as a spiritual exercise.

FIG. 9—Place the palms together and spread the fingers. Interlock the digits and close them so the fingers rest on the backs of the hands. The thumbs are placed side by side, resting on the first knuckle of the index fingers. Lift the hands and hold them in front of the body.

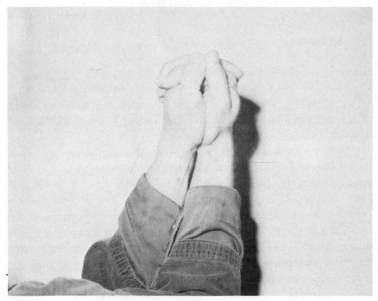

FIG. 9

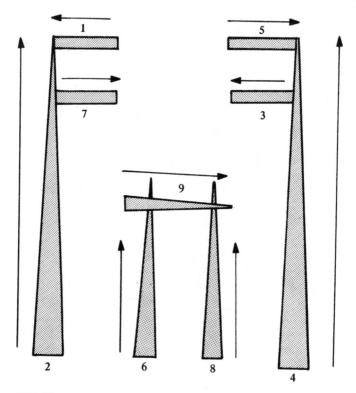

FIG. 10

FIG. 10—Using the thumbs as a pointer, describe the ideogram as before. Close the eyes and visualize the character. You will feel the beat of the pulse in the palms and the Chi flowing in the arms. Place the hands in the lap.

Hold the head erect, exhale, emptying the lungs from top to bottom. Turn the head to look over the left shoulder and inhale, filling the lungs from bottom to top. Turn the head to face forward and exhale. Turn the head to look over the right shoulder and inhale as before. Turn the head to face front and exhale. This completes one round. Repeat this exercise eighty-one times. The tongue should be placed lightly against the roof of the mouth during this exercise. On the eighty-first repetition, having faced forward and exhaled, maintain the position and inhale once more. Imagine the breath being drawn into the lower abdomen, warming the region. When you feel this warmth, breathe out slowly and relax the body.

The Yang Yu (Wei Mo) in the arms links the shoulders with the center of the palms after passing through the middle fingers. The Dragon Cavity of the hand is located by bending the middle finger of the left hand into the palm. Where it touches is a spot which is linked with the heart and lower abdomen by an artery passing through the left wrist. The Tiger Cavity is found by bending the middle finger of the right hand into the palm. Where this touches, the heart and lower abdomen are linked by a vein passing through the right wrist. These are now charged with Chi. The practice of Kuji Kiri is the art of transmitting this energy.

The Hara is the key to the first two centers of the body. Only at this stage can true meditation be achieved. The first exercise, Chu, developed the power of sensory withdrawal; the second, Shen, developed the power of concentration; this, the third, develops meditative ability.

To make the distinction between this level and the preceding two, an element of duration is introduced. Concentration can be held only for a certain length of time, depending on the individual. At the end of this period, it either becomes meditation, in which the gross aspects of the universe dissolve into their subtler components; or the concentration is voluntarily broken. If the former occurs, the student enters a somnolent state, neither awake nor asleep, yet totally relaxed. One of the results of this relaxation is the diminution of effort and the progressive disappearance of the will. To relax is to passively withdraw into ourselves, to become one with the universe. This is sometimes known as a state of trance contemplation.

TAI (FOURTH KANJI)

The fourth center of power in the body is located at the site of the navel. The channel of energy which flows from this point is known as the *Tai Mo*, or Belt Channel, and passes around both sides of the body, encircling the belly. If it is not functioning properly the belly will be distended and the waist will feel cool and wet. Loss of appetite is another symptom. This center is concerned with digestive functions, its counterpart is the solar plexus. It represents the fire element, its form is triangular. This level is characterized by spirit and the successful conclusion of the meditation. In this state, the mind becomes one with the object of meditation, together with the concept and the name of the object. In combat, the *kiai*, or spirit shout, is drawn from this source.

FIG. 11—To form the kanji, place the hands back to back, fingers pointing down. Spread the fingers and interlock them from within. Bring the elbows down, bringing the palms together over the fingers, en-

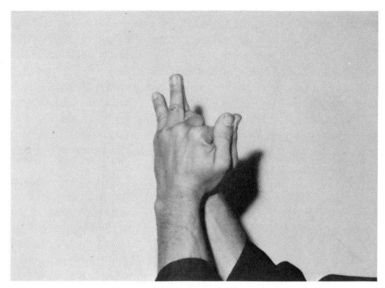

FIG. 11

closing them within the hands. Extricate the ring and little fingers and extend them with the tips touching. The thumbs are extended and pointing toward the body.

FIG. 12—Lift the hands in front of the body and describe the illustrated ideogram by alternately drawing five horizontal and four vertical lines using the tips of the little fingers as a pointer. Visualize this character.

Hold the head erect, facing forward with the eyes closed. The tip of the tongue is held lightly between the lips and the mouth is slightly open. Inhale through the mouth, producing a wheezing sound and filling the lungs from bottom to top. When the inhalation is complete, close the mouth. Tilt the head to the right side as if to place the right ear on the shoulder. The neck does not twist during this movement. Hold this position for nine heartbeats. Return the head to an upright position, exhale through the nose. Part the lips slightly and inhale through the mouth as before. Tilt the left ear to the left shoulder and retain the breath for nine heartbeats. Return the head to an upright position and exhale through the nose. Repeat this exercise eighty-one times. This develops the spirit.

This exercise begins a second phase in breathing techniques. The first three exercises involved creating an oxygen debt, making the system more acidic, and were concerned with the accumulation of energy. The next three are designed to saturate the blood stream with oxygen,

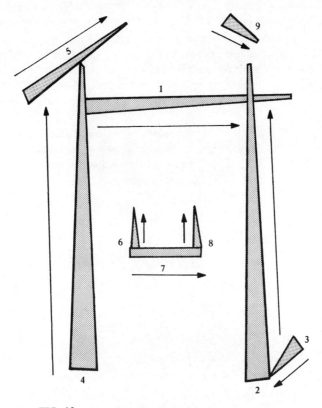

FIG. 12

making the system more alkaline; these are concerned with the direction of energy. These are characterized by the breezy sensation felt on the tongue during the performance of this exercise.

The last three exercises are concerned with the transmission of energy.

SHA (FIFTH KANJI)

The fifth center of power is located at the solar plexus. It represents the air element and is symbolized by two triangles—one facing up, the other down. Its color is smoky. This center controls respiration. The channel known as the *Ch'ueng Mo,* or Thrusting Channel, ends at the heart, or solar plexus, having begun between the Jen Mo and the Tu Mo at the genitals. If this channel is not functioning properly, disorders of the digestive system will be seen. The base of the Eight Psychic Channels is the Gate of Mortality at the root of the genitals.

This is connected to the base of the spine by the Tu Mo, which in turn is linked with the Jen Mo in the brain. From there, the channel passes through the center of the head to the palate, or Heavenly Pool, where the Chi is collected and allowed to escape during meditation. Beneath the palate, the channel passes behind the throat, through the pulmonary artery and hepatic artery, past the diaphragm, behind the solar plexus, below the navel, and back to the genitals. In this way the Chi flows through the body.

FIG. 13—Form the kanji by placing the hands back to back and interlocking the fingers inside as before. This time, withdraw the first and little fingers and join them at the finger tips. Extend the thumbs side by side as before, facing toward the body.

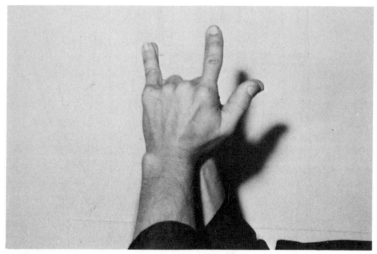

FIG. 13

FIG. 14—Describe the illustrated figure for visualization as before, using the index fingers. Place the hands in the lap.

Hold the head erect, facing forward with the eyes closed. Place the tip of the tongue against the roof of the mouth. Inhale and exhale through the nose as quickly and fully as possible eighty-one times. This supersaturates the blood stream with oxygen. On the eighty-first inhalation, hold the breath with the diaphragm. Retain this inhalation for eighty-one heartbeats. You will feel the beat of your pulse in the temples. This exercise develops the power to relieve pain through psychic means.

The yogic concept of prana is useful in understanding this. *Prana* is not the consciousness or the spirit, but is merely the energy used by the

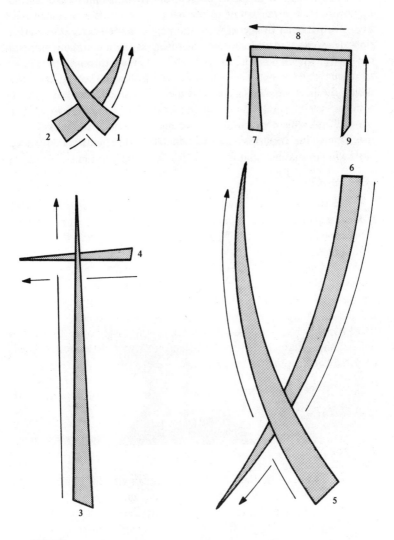

FIG. 14

soul in its material and astral manifestations. Prana is in the air, but it is not the oxygen; it is in food, but is not the chemical components. It is absorbed by the body during respiration. One who can learn to control this pranic energy has the power to bring it to a state of vibration that can be conveyed to others, causing them to vibrate harmonically. He who has abundant pranic energy radiates strength and health.

When healing with pranic energy, the physician must take care not to transmit his own energy to the patient; rather, the physician must draw the patient's own energy and direct it to the source of the affliction. The source may be obscure at times, as there are many points of the body which may be invaded by illness, and many which are attacked by excesses. There is only one sure method of diagnosis: taking the pulses in the Chinese manner. This practice in itself calls for a subjective interpretation on the part of the physician. A wise physician will take his own pulse first, to insure his own calmness; he will also cleanse his mind after an examination, so that his previous diagnosis will not bias his findings.

JEN (SIXTH KANJI)

The sixth center of power is located behind the throat. It controls speech and hearing, and corresponds to the pharangeal plexus. Its element is air, its color is the shade of pure sea water. From the heel, the *Yang Chiao*, or Positive Leg Channel, rises along the outer sides of the ankles and legs, up the sides of the body, around the head, and down below the ear, ending at the sixth center. If this channel is not functioning properly, one will be unable to sleep. Also, disorders arising from imbalance, paralysis, weakness, and lethargy will be noted.

FIG. 15—Form the kanji by placing the hands back to back as before, and interlocking the fingers inside. This time keep the fingers enclosed between the palms, extending none.

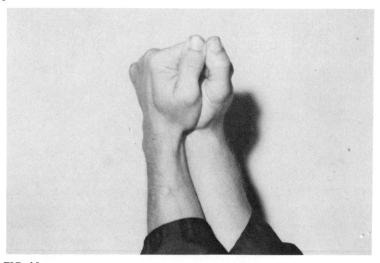

FIG. 15

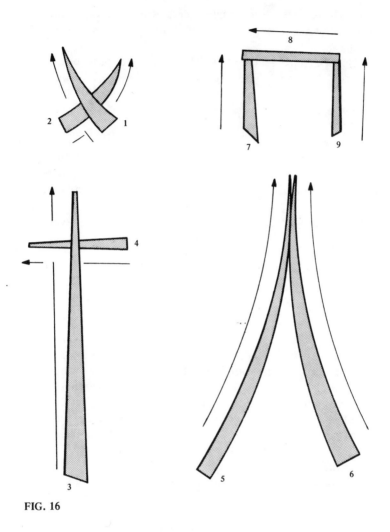

FIG. 16

FIG. 16—Describe the illustrated figure by tracing five horizontal and four vertical lines for visualization, using the thumbs (knuckle) as a pointer. Place the hands in the lap.

Hold the head erect, facing forward, with the eyes closed. Inhale deeply and fully through the nose, filling the lungs from bottom to top. The tongue should be placed lightly against the roof of the mouth. Exhale through the nose as you hum, vibrating the palate and stimulating the Heavenly Pool. Empty the lungs from top to bottom. This causes the exhalation to be extended beyond the inhalation, and causes the exhalation to be more complete. Because of the depth of the breath taken, the blood becomes more alkaline. Repeat this movement eighty-one times.

This technique sometimes involves the yogic *Aum* to extend the exhalation. It develops the psychic sense of hearing allowing one to hear the inner voice. Further, it stimulates the proximity sense which allows one to feel the presence of the enemy and locate him in total darkness.

At this stage of meditation, the object of concentration loses its associations with either name or concept; the object is simply the object. The meditator comes to differentiate between the dimensions of reality and those of the mind and gains access to the inner knowledge.

This center controls all of the automatic body functions ruled by the cephalic region of the brain. It also serves as the psychic force which separates the astral body from the physical at the time of death. Meditation on this center leads to the philosophical concept of oneself—"I am that I am."

TUNG (SEVENTH KANJI)

The seventh center of power is located at the site of the third eye, slightly above and between the eyebrows. The *Yin Chiao*, or Negative Leg Channel, rises from the instep through the inner leg, past the scrotum, up the center of the body, to this spot. If this channel is not functioning properly, one will sleep too much. This center represents the highest level of mind. Meditation on this site enables one to gain control over the various nerve centers of the body. Here also the astral counterpart of the sensory and motor nerve fibers of the spinal column converge. Along these travel the nerve impulses which control the body. In yoga this site is known as *Triveni*, or Three Knots.

One will also note an extraordinary spiritual strength, knowledge, and will power. This center is the seat of the force in the body. Its color is snow-white, its shape is triangular. The acquisition of the higher voice, or intuitional knowledge and clairvoyance, resides at this center, as does the soul. It is here that the Ninja directs his Chi at the time of death.

With continued practice, the serpent power of the first center rises, not to this level, but to the next, the cortical surface of the brain. This is sometimes referred to as the Thousand Petal Lotus.

Each of the centers so far experienced is also a center of consciousness which may be activated by the sound energy of a chant or by meditation. For each center there is a specific chant, and for each a specific mandala in the form of the visualized ideogram. By these means, the force may be channeled to perform the will. The passage of the serpent power from the lowest to the site of the seventh center constitutes the first third of the journey. From here the energy rises to the Lotus and merges with the consciousness of the Infinite. At this level, one overcomes the limits of time and space, and gains the ability to control the actions of others without physical contact.

FIG. 17–Place the hands, palms together, fingers pointing upward. Fold the fingers of the left hand, leaving the index finger extended. Wrap the fingers of the right fist around the extended left finger and press the right thumbnail against the side of the left index fingernail at the point where the cuticle ends. You will know when you are pressing the right point; it will feel like a mild electric shock. This pinches off the flow of energy in the body and recirculates it through the Yin and Yang Wei Mo to the solar plexus, and hence to the third eye.

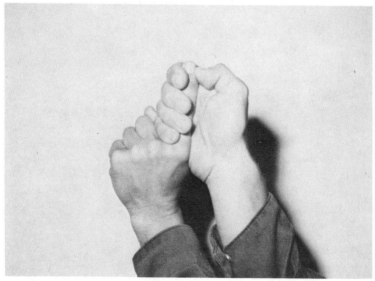

FIG. 17

FIG. 18–Describe the illustrated ideogram as before, using the tip of the left finger.

From this level on, only proper breathing techniques are employed. This consists of inhaling through the nose for a period of four heartbeats, holding the inhalation with the diaphragm for two beats, exhaling for four beats, and holding the exhalation for two beats. This completes one round of the Fourfold Breath. The tip of the tongue remains lightly against the roof of the mouth. Repeat this exercise eighty-one times. If you are meditating with a chant for a specific center, the ex-

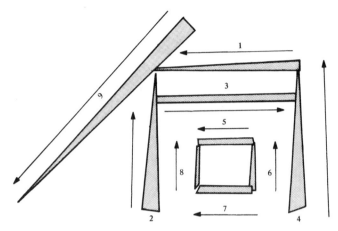

FIG. 18

halation will be performed through the mouth while forming the appropriate sound. It should be no longer than four heartbeats.

Only when the inner force has been consciously directed to this site can it be said that one has achieved success in controlling and manipulating the serpent power, which then appears as a flash of lightning. Even to reach this state requires at least nine years of hard work following the method and contemplation of one's Sensei.

The serious student is admonished again that the true power cannot be awakened without long and steady practice, and then is not given to one without the proper moral credentials to employ it.

Beware of those who would make you a master overnight. A true teacher never expects anything of his students, and awaits the proper time to teach everything.

HUA (EIGHTH KANJI)

The eighth center of power is located on the cortical surface of the brain. It is known as the Thousand Petal Lotus because, when visualized, this is the imagery created. When the Chi permeates this center, the sensation in the body is one of floating upward to the surface, much like the blossoming of the lotus.

When the serpent power passes from the lowest center through the psychic channels and junctions to this level, the energy in these begins to spin as each is opened. At this time the marriage of spirit and matter occurs, and the individual consciousness unites with the universal consciousness. This is a state of ultimate bliss, rarely achieved even by those who practice a lifetime.

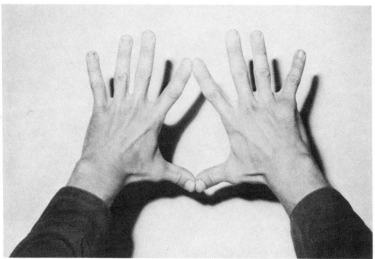

FIG. 19

The ascending practices for this and the next level are achieved through specific exercises which are similar to those given for the first seven centers. These are always given verbally by master to student. They cannot and should not be described. Let it be sufficient to state that the finger-knitting kanji illustrated (see **FIG. 19** and **FIG. 20**) represents the suffusion of the conscious into the Infinite, and enables the practitioner to exercise his will through the five elements.

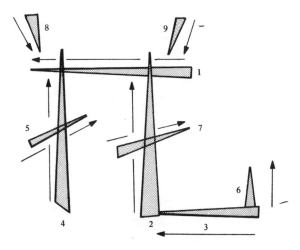

FIG. 20

FIG. 21

TAO (NINTH KANJI)

The ninth center of power is the aura of the body. The *aura* consists of an electromagnetic field surrounding the physical self, radiating in all directions. The strength and extent of the field are determined by the individual. The kanji represents the acquisition of the secret knowledge. (Refer to **FIG. 21** and **FIG. 22** for hand position and ideogram.)

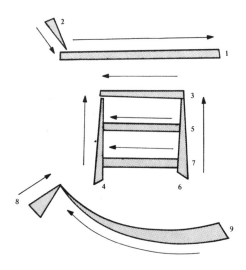

FIG. 22

To become a Ninja, one must accomplish four things: *one must be strong; one must know; one must dare; and one must be silent.* It was said of the ancient Ninja that he could become invisible at will. This may be the myth and legend of a bygone era; it may be that simple tricks and ruses led to this belief; or it may be that the Ninja of old could actually alter the state of his aura and the surrounding atmosphere by physiopsychic means, rendering himself unseeable. One skilled in this technique would, quite naturally, be reluctant to demonstrate it, and would certainly never reveal his method to the uninitiated. This art is sometimes known in Kuji Kiri as "the power to cloud men's minds."

Remember, the Tao that can be told is not the eternal Tao. It cannot be explained, but it can be experienced. This is the goal of meditation.

TRANSITORY EXERCISES

Just as one cannot plunge headlong into the practice of *Chi Kung* (breathing exercises), one cannot return to the real world from such an experience without some transitory phase. The ancients have taught the following movements to calm the mind and body and return them to a more balanced condition before the conclusion of the exercise. Suddenly standing after any of the preceding techniques would almost certainly result in the blood rushing from the head, causing one to faint before the heart can compensate.

FIG. 23—Extend the left arm out to the side. Bend the arm at the elbow and rotate the arm in a circular manner counterclockwise thirty-six times. Repeat this action with the right arm. This stimulates the Yang Yu and Yin Yu channels of the arm.

FIG. 24—Lift the left leg off the right hip and extend it in front of the body; lift the right leg off the left hip and extend it. This releases

FIG. 23   **FIG. 24**

the Lotus position. Clasp the hands together and raise the arms above the head, turning the palms over as they pass the face. Inhale as the hands ascend from the lap to the head, and exhale as you push upward. Repeat this movement nine times.

FIG. 25—Place the palms on the sides of the legs just below the hips. Stretch the legs and slide the palms down the sides of the thighs, knees, and calves. Bend the body forward and touch the head to the knees while grasping the outside of the feet with both palms. Inhale as you return to a sitting position, and exhale as you bend forward. Repeat this movement twelve times. This will stimulate the legs and keep them straight.

FIG. 25

With the completion of the transitory exercises (FIG. 26), the meditator has accomplished the basic movements of the first nine Mind Gates. These must be mastered before one can even attempt those which deal with the more specific techniques of the acupuncture meridians, the four seas of the body, the six solid and the six empty organs, and so on.

FIG. 26

CENTERS OF POWER (GLOSSARY)

Chu–*pillar*. In Chinese medicine, the spine is often referred to as the Heavenly Pillar of the body.

Shen–*body*. This refers to the Gate of Mortality, whence comes the body.

Kai–*open*. This center is the key to all the others. Once this has been experienced, the rest is easy.

Tai–*belt*. This is the only latitudinal channel of the body, separating it into the upper and lower quadrants.

Sha–*to die*. The Ninja say that death always comes from the left side and that once it is upon you, the pounding of the heart is felt. When the heart stops, the body begins to die.

Jen–*man*. This refers to man as a species. Since man is the only known animal with a systematic spoken language, this center separates the human from the beast.

Tung–*understand*. This center corresponds to the cavernous plexus. Once this level is reached, enlightenment cannot be far beyond.

Hua–*flower*. This refers to the concept of the Thousand Petal Lotus.

Tao–*path* or *way*. Do not be confused by this translation. The path is not one which leads to a true goal, but rather to an understanding of the path itself. *Seek not to know all the answers, but rather to understand the questions.*

3 The Art Of Hiding

Inpo, the Art of Hiding, is an integral part of the Ninjitsu system. It simply means that one must take advantage of every possible object, natural as well as manmade, to conceal oneself. Inpo gave rise to the legends that the ancient Ninja could vanish at will.

Foremost among the precepts of Inpo is the admonition to avoid unnecessary movement. The Ninja employs this in conjunction with the principle of *Monomi-no-jitsu,* or "observing the enemy from his perimeter." Following are the five preferred Inpo methods:

EARTH METHOD

The best example of this technique is supplied by *Uzura gakure no-jitsu,* which suggests hiding like a quail in small gaps between two larger objects. The primary consideration here is that one must be able to completely fill the space between the objects. In this way, one may escape detection, since an observer will scan past these as he walks his post. Of note also is the technique of hiding under overhanging brush or grass. Stay low to observe and look around the cover.

AIR METHOD

This refers to hiding like a raccoon, *Tanuki gakure no-jitsu.* It means that one should climb a tree or other high place and press oneself against the object so that one seems to be a part of it. The infamous jewel thieves, Alan Kuhn and Jack Murphy—who stole the Star of India from a New York museum—made frequent use of this tactic. They believed, and rightly so, that people seldom look up.

WATER METHOD

Sometimes known as *Kitsune gakure no-jitsu,* this means to imitate the actions of the fox by concealing oneself in water. Not only does this aid in erasing one's trail, but also allows only poor footing for the pursuing enemy. A variation is the *Tanuki* method of dragging the enemy into the water for the purpose of drowning him.

FIRE METHOD

This is perhaps the most difficult of the Inpo arts. It refers to the erasing of sound and shadow. Always move behind a light source to avoid casting a shadow which might betray you. Learn to move silently. Only practice in the Nine Steps can develop this skill. (See chapter on Kuji Ashi.)

WOOD METHOD

Pu Neng Mu is the term used to mean "invisibility in plain sight." When no cover is at hand, one must hide behind nothing. This is accomplished by distorting the silhouette. It is possible to form the body into many shapes by means of yogic exercises. In the old days of Ninjitsu, one excellent tactic involved replacing a scarecrow and standing in the center of a plowed field. By kneeling and wrapping the arms around the knees, one assumes a rounded posture. This is known as "hiding like a stone."

Numerous other methods exist for concealing one's presence from the enemy, such as disguises, mingling with crowds, false identities, and so on. These alternatives lie in the realm of strategical, rather than tactical considerations, and have been omitted here as they do not relate directly to penetration of the enemy encampment.

INTELLIGENCE GATHERING

To be successful, one must obtain every available scrap of intelligence about the size, location, and logistics of the enemy base. This may be accomplished in many ways. However, once the site has been reached, firsthand data is readily obtainable and absolutely essential.

No one knows the territory quite like the one who has been there and back. Once in the field, the Ninja alone can determine the feasibility of the mission. He does this by observing. The art of Ninjitsu *is* invisibility. Nowhere else is it more evident than in this phase of Inpo.

Having selected a site from which to study the enemy, assume whatever posture is required for maximum cover, concealment, and comfort. You must have a clear field of view, preferably with your back to cover. Select a point for penetration into the enemy camp and fix your eyes upon it. Inhale deeply and slowly, filling the lungs from bottom to top. Close the eyes and exhale fully and slowly, using the technique known as *T'an Hsi* (sighing). Tense the Hara (the seat of breathing) slightly, inhale as before. Exhale, visualizing the character *san* (a Chinese ideogram consisting of three horizontal lines one above another) three times. Inhale, exhale and visualize the character *erh* (Chinese ideogram of two lines) three times. Inhale, exhale and visualize the character *tan* (a single horizontal line) three times. Holding this exhalation with the diaphragm, visualize the point of penetration for five to ten seconds (nine heartbeats). Inhale slowly, tasting the air. Care must be taken at this juncture not to gulp air and reveal the position. Relax the Hara. Relax the body. Open the eyes slowly. Breathe slowly, deeply, and naturally. Scan the enemy camp. Do this for at least an hour. This is known as *Kuji Kiri* (meditation).

At first it will be difficult to keep the attention focused on the enemy camp; with practice it will be easier. When gazing at one spot for an extended period, the eyes become fatigued. Then the muscles relax and the eye wanders naturally. It is during this period that the patterns and routines of the camp may be observed.

Great attention should be placed on the breathing initially. During stress the heartbeat speeds up and it is possible to soon be breathing audibly without realizing it. Listen for the sound of your own heartbeat; this will reassure you.

This breathing technique is used naturally by hunters. When combined with certain finger-knitting exercises, as well as yogic postures and other methods of breathing, a system known as the Nine Forms of the Mind Gate *(Hsi Men Jitsu)* is formed. Each of these has evolved nine variations, making a total of eighty-one forms.

When moving from your position to advance on the enemy, the body will feel light, as though in a dream. Silence is essential.

INDIVIDUAL MOVEMENT

Having observed the enemy camp and confirmed, denied, or discovered sufficient intelligence to plan ingress and egress of the site, select a route and proceed.

Since these operations will be conducted alone and often at night, consider any condition which might provide an advantage. One noteworthy condition is the weather. Rainy nights are best. Moonless nights are second best. In warmer seasons, insects, frogs, and nocturnal predators may draw attention to your position by ceasing their nightly songs. In winter, the clear, crisp air often carries the slightest sound to an alert sentry.

There are nine specific times when the enemy is most vulnerable:

1) The night before the enemy is ready. This means that the enemy is aware of an impending attack, but his spies believe the enemy is at least a day away.

2) The night after the enemy has heavily fortified his position. The physical labor will tire the enemy soldiers.

3) The night the enemy sends out patrols. This takes advantage of the enemy mistaking any sounds you might make as those of his returning patrols.

4) The night after the enemy has sustained heavy losses. This is known as "harrying the retreat."

5) The night the enemy prepares to counterattack. This means that the enemy is anticipating the next day's conflict. The Ninja takes advantage of this anxiety.

6) The night after the siege has been lifted. The enemy will relax at this time.

7) The night the enemy is struck with sickness, hunger, or thirst. The enemy will be weakened by these.

8) Any night after the enemy has been wearied by a long, fruitless confrontation. The enemy will be disheartened.

9) The night after an enemy victory. The enemy will be triumphant and let his guard down. This is known as a "spoiling mission."

Penetration of the enemy camp is hindered by two things: barriers and sentries. The first of these may be overcome by utilizing the techniques shown herein. Sentries must be circumvented or assassinated. Sentry removal techniques will be explained in a later section.

Remember, an enemy can see you only as well as you can see him. In all probability, you can see him better.

MOVEMENT RULES

Follow these general rules to move without being seen or heard by the enemy:

- Camouflage yourself and your equipment.
- Wear soft, well-fitting clothes. Starched clothing swishes, baggy clothing is likely to snag.

- Use ankle ties to blouse the trousers. Do not tie them too tightly as this retards circulation.
- Do not carry unnecessary equipment.
- Look for your next point of concealment before leaving your position.
- Change direction when moving through tall grass; a straight path causes an unnatural motion which attracts attention.
- If you alarm birds or animals, remain in one position and observe. Their flight may attract attention.
- Take advantage of distractions provided by natural noises.
- Cross roads and trails where maximum cover exists, look for a low spot or curve, cross quickly and silently.
- Follow the furrows when crawling over a plowed field, crossing the furrows at low spots.
- Avoid steep slopes and areas with loose gravel or stones.
- Avoid cleared areas and prevent silhouetting.
- Avoid heavily trafficked areas.
- Avoid areas which are not trafficked at all. They may be mined or booby-trapped.
- Always move downwind from kennels or guard-dog positions.
- Observe the enemy as much as possible, watching for indications that you have been discovered.
- When in doubt, do not move.
- Learn the patterns used to see, that you may move outside the field of view.
- Learn to move without disturbing your surroundings.

In these you must research and train diligently.

4 The Nine Steps

Man sees in three ways, by movement, silhouette, and color. Man also hears, and some hear more acutely than others. Also, since masters can sense an alien presence, one must have a calm mind to escape their notice. To elude all these sensory pickups is *to be invisible* for all practical purposes.

To eradicate color, the Ninja employs black art, a magician's skill. Black is the absence of color. This means that a black surface absorbs all of the light rays incident upon it, reflecting none. It is the reflected rays that give an object its apparent color. Further, a black surface casts no shadow upon itself to define its depth.

To distort the silhouette, one employs yogic postures and camouflage. An example is the *kimono-ninja* technique. The cape may be draped over the body in a variety of manners to alter shape, or the kimono may be arranged independently to make it appear that one is standing where one is not. This is called *Ametori no-jitsu.*

To erase shadow and sound, the Ninja uses the Nine Steps detailed next.

HAI PU (BLACK/STEALTHY STEP)

First among the Kuji Ashi is the *Hai Pu,* the Black/Stealthy Step. It is taught not only as a means of moving in total darkness, but also as a type of dynamic meditation. In its advancing and retreating action is the core of Ninjitsu. Only by this method can one develop the kinesthetic sense of the body that is required to practice Ninjitsu. Master Hai Pu first.

This technique is used in total darkness. It is designed for the protection of the body, for moving silently and slowly, and for attacking instantly.

FIG. 27—Assume the following stance: lower the hips and raise both arms; the feet should be one shoulder's width apart; turn the toes inward; bend the knees and lower the hips until the knees touch. The hips are back, the shoulders shrugged, the head is lowered. Draw the elbows close to the chest, raise the hands above the head and extend the fingers. The eyes are directed without being fixed at a spot on the path about ten feet away. Martial artists will recognize this as a variation of the closed stance of Praying Mantis Kung Fu.

FIG. 28—Keeping the hips and shoulders at the same level, shift the weight onto the right leg; glide the left toes forward and out in a semicircular manner, keeping the knees together. The body does not move above the hips, but gently weaves from side to side as weight is shifted over each foot alternately.

FIG. 28a—The right foot is then drawn over to the left ankle in the loose-ankle step of *T'ai Chi Chuan,* and advanced in a similar manner. Practice in this step strengthens the hips and feet, developing balance. The most important point in practicing this step is that the hips and shoulders do not change their level. The arms act as antennae, sensing obstacles, and protecting the head. Practice in this step develops an unconscious awareness of the body as a whole.

In kabuki theater, this technique is performed so slowly that even though the Ninja remains in plain view, no movement is discernible. In ancient times, this method was used in *crossing the obi,* or sash-belt. If confronted by a gravel path or a nightingale floor (one designed to creak when weight is applied), the Ninja would roll his obi across the obstacle and tread its narrow width, effectively muffling any sound which might betray him.

Practice moving forward about ten feet, then back, always directing the Chi forward.

HENG PU (CROSS STEP)

The second of the Nine Steps to learn is the *Heng Pu.* By employing this technique, it is possible to move quickly and quietly in narrow passages, corridors, and hallways. In combat, this stance presents a smaller silhouette to the enemy. Also, when fleeing, one presents a smaller target. Note that tracks left by this method appear to travel in two directions at once.

Much of the actual penetration of the enemy camp will involve traversing narrow alleys between buildings, or flattening against a wall

FIG. 27

FIG. 28

FIG. 28 a

to remain concealed in its shadow. This requires a posture which overcomes the width of the shoulders. In order to move forward, one must move sideways.

FIG. 29—To assume this stance, stand with back to the wall, crouch slightly, bow the legs with knees pointing out, turn the head in the direction you wish to move and lower the shoulder facing that direction. This is an exaggerated fencing posture, with the lead toe at a 90-degree angle to the body and the rear foot facing 135 degrees away from it.

FIG. 30—Now cross-step in back with the rear leg, placing the toes past the lead foot, facing in their original direction. The toes of each foot now face those of the other. This extreme toe-in position is necessary to allow clearance for the lead leg which is drawn through as weight is shifted onto the rear leg. Step out with the lead leg to again assume the original position.

FIG. 31—Having developed some skill in this technique, begin to practice the Cross Step in front. Each of these has its uses and applications. Bear in mind the importance of the toe-in position during this exercise as well.

FIG. 29   **FIG. 30**   **FIG. 31**

FIG. 32   FIG. 33   FIG. 34

FIG. 32–The eyes scan the ground about three yards in front of the feet. Care must be taken not to look toward the enemy when moving, as the face may reflect moonlight and the eyes will shine if struck directly by a strong light. Further, obstacles which may lie in the path (stones, trip wires, etc.) are more readily visible. Using the eyes in this manner takes advantage of pupil dilation. When looking ahead, the pupils contract as light enters the eye. By focusing on the path, less light enters the eye. The pupils expand and more is seen through the rod cells, resulting in a type of off-center vision.

FIG. 33–The Heng Pu is easily mastered and enables one to move quickly over great distances, making no sound, with little fatigue. Practice by moving flat along a wall without touching it. The step should be at least one yard per pace, at the speed of a double-quick march. Once this level has been achieved, crouch lower. This strengthens the legs and makes it possible to move quickly in low shadows and under windows.

FIG. 34–When passing a window in this manner, it is advisable to listen for sounds from inside. Should the occupants be silent or snoring, or be engaged in an activity which requires their attention, they are less likely to detect your presence. One should listen at both sides, before and after passing.

FIG. 35 FIG. 36

P'A PU (NIGHT WALKING ABILITY)

Third among the Nine Steps is *P'a Pu,* or Night Walking Ability. This movement is developed by running on the balls of the feet. After much practice, add weight to the ankles. This strengthens the feet, making it possible to walk on tiptoe for great distances. This aids in eliminating sound.

FIG. 35—P'a Pu is employed when it is necessary to move quietly and quickly forward. Exhale and tense the Hara. Lower the body for better balance. Extend the arms, palms down, at waist level. Step forward with the left foot first, balancing on the right leg. Place the toes lightly on the surface, and shift body weight forward.

FIG. 36—As you move over the left foot, draw the toes back slightly, press the left heel down lightly. Glide forward, advancing the right foot in a similar manner. It will be noted that this is a variation of the hunting step, in which the toes may be used to clear leaves, twigs, and other small debris from the path before stepping on them.

SHE PU (SERPENT STEP)

The fourth technique is called *She Pu,* the Serpent Step. It is so named because the action of the Ninja's body resembles that of a snake. She Pu is used at times when one must move close to the ground to avoid being discovered. Use She Pu when cover is scarce, visibility permits good enemy observation, and speed is not essential.

FIG. 37—Keep the body as flat as possible. The hands are kept palms down, near the face, with elbows close to the body, legs spread, and toes outward. The head is lifted to observe the enemy. Study the movements of a stalking cat to perfect this approach. To move forward, extend the arms and draw the left leg forward. Pull with the arms and the toes of the left foot. The weight is borne on the forearms and the left leg from knee to ankle. Thus, the body is lifted slightly above the ground to prevent scraping or dragging noises. Change the pushing leg frequently to avoid fatigue. Stop, listen, and observe after each movement. Silence and slow movement are essential.

FIG. 37

FIG. 38

LUNG PU (DRAGON STEP)

The Dragon Step is a variation of the Serpent Step. Use the Lung Pu technique when cover and concealment are available, when poor visibility reduces enemy watchfulness, and when more speed is needed.

FIG. 38—Keep the body free of the ground by resting body weight on the forearms and lower legs. The knees are maintained low behind the buttocks to reduce silhouette. Move forward by alternately advancing the right knee/left elbow and the left knee/right elbow. For the most part, sounds made by these motions are muffled by the costume. However, in this position one is quite vulnerable. It is therefore recommended for use in the primary ingress phase, which is beyond the enemy reach, but not beyond his field of view.

T'U PU (RUSHING STEP)

The Kuji Ashi's fifth step, *T'u Pu,* is the fastest way to move from one point of concealment to another. Unfortunately, it also exposes one to enemy observation. The Rushing Step is employed only when sufficient background exists to prevent silhouetting.

FIG. 39—From the prone position, slowly raise the head and select your next point of concealment. Lower the head, draw the arms into the body, keeping the elbows in, and pull the right leg forward. In one movement, raise the body by straightening the arms. Spring to the feet, stepping off with the left foot first.

FIG. 40—Run to the new position using the shortest route. Carry the body on the balls of the feet, in a crouch, with the shoulders rounded, arms hanging loosely at knee level. Press the first knuckle of each index finger with the ball of the thumb. The fingers are thus curled loosely and are carried as though the hands were sliding along a rail. This is known as *P'ao Nei An,* or "running in darkness."

As you near the next position, plant the feet slightly apart, drop to the knees as quietly as possible, fall forward and break the impact with the heels of the hands. Shift your weight to either side and roll over into position behind cover. Lie as flat as possible. If you think your movement was observed, move to the right or left as cover permits.

FIG. 39

FIG. 40

JU MEN PU (ENTERING PIVOT)

The sixth step is the *Ju Men Pu,* or Entering Pivot. This consists of a short retreat, heel first, without shifting the body weight. It is also the basis for the *Huo Nei Kuo* (Capture by Passing) of Tonpo. Practice is most effective when turning the corner.

FIG. 41—Approach the barrier, press against it, resting the weight forward. Place the near hand by the knee and the back hand close to the face. Slowly lean the head forward and peek around the corner. The lower this is done, the smaller the chances are of being observed.

FIG. 42—Having determined that movement can be accomplished safely, draw the head back out of sight. Step quickly around the corner with the lead foot (in this case the left), placing the heel in the final position shown. The right leg does not move at this point, thus placing one in a wide Horse Stance diagonally against the edge of the building. The back glides around the corner without touching it as the weight is shifted onto the left leg. When the hips have cleared the wall, the right leg is drawn around to close the stance. Press your back to the wall and check to see that this action was not seen before proceeding.

FIG. 41   **FIG. 42**

CH'IANG PI KUNG (WALL CLIMBING ABILITY)

Two things hinder penetration of the enemy camp: barriers and sentries. To overcome the first of these, the Ninja employs the seventh step, *Ch'iang Pi Kung,* his Wall Climbing Ability. This consists of making the body light, and advancing in accordance with the theory of opposition. That theory states that maximum balance is obtained by moving the opposite arm and leg simultaneously as in the Lung Pu, Dragon Step.

FIG. 43—Ancient texts tell of a method using the elbows and heels to climb with the back to the wall, as illustrated. This technique requires three years' practice crawling on the floor, three years' climbing on a wall with bricks jutting out, and three years' climbing on a smooth wall. Movement by this method may be vertical, horizontal, or diagonal.

Climbing by these means may be accomplished by employing any ornamental ledge or windowsill. A lip of one inch for each point of contact (finger tips, toes) is sufficient for this purpose if sufficient finger strength can be generated.

FIG. 44—Press the body against the surface, getting a feel for the wall's material. Look directly upward, selecting the handhold route you will employ. Grip the ledge, and place the toes on a second ledge or other projection.

FIG. 43   **FIG. 44**

FIG. 45   **FIG. 46**

FIG. 45—Simultaneously push with the legs and pull with the arms, gaining sufficient momentum to carry your hand to the edge of the wall. Maintain your balance by means of the other three points of contact. Only one such point is moved at a time in this technique.

FIG. 46—Shift the other hand to the wall edge and, using the arms to bear most of your weight, advance the legs alternately until you gain the summit. Once there, lie flat and listen for sounds denoting that you were observed. It is essential when moving on rooftops to avoid silhouetting. Therefore, the steeper the angle of the roof, the more one must hug its surface.

FIG. 47—Walls may be ascended with the chest to the surface, using drainpipes or trellises, bearing in mind that these are considerably weaker at the top than at the base. Test the structure by grasping it firmly with both hands and pulling straight down, exerting a steadily increasing pressure until you can lift your body to the toes. Gently push and pull against the supports which anchor the pipe before starting the climb.

FIG. 47

FIG. 49

FIG. 48   FIG. 50

FIG. 48–When confronted by a fence topped by barbed wire, three methods may be used to cross this perimeter. First, you may climb the barrier, finding ample hand and footholds near the support poles. It is best to support body weight with the arms, staying as parallel to the fence as possible.

FIG. 49–When crossing the barbed wire, grasp it either at the support, or between the barbs and slowly let yourself over, taking care not to snag the uniform.

FIG. 50–Drop to the ground clear of the fence's other side. Land evenly on the feet, executing a forward roll immediately to absorb your impact and carry you away behind a preselected point of concealment.

The second method is to cut the wire. The best way to do this is to make a slit vertically, severing as few links as possible, until the mesh can be spread like a zipper, allowing you to pass.

The third is to burrow under the fence, in the manner of a dog tunneling to freedom. Both methods, however, leave evidence of your passing and are not true to the principles of Ninjitsu.

A final note: care must be taken not to touch electrified barriers. Look for bare wire attached at intervals to insulators, or small dead animals which have inadvertently touched the fence. Most commercial installations clearly mark electrified fences to prevent accidental injuries.

FIG. 51   FIG. 52   FIG. 53

PIEN PU (SIDE STEP)

Eighth among the Kuji Ashi is the *Pien Pu,* or Side Step. Though similar to the Heng Pu (Cross Step) in that movement is directed to the side, Pien Pu is employed to move more slowly in narrow spaces. Its best use comes when passing through a threshold, such as a door.

FIG. 51—Press your shoulder to the wall, placing the lead hand near the hip and the rear hand near the shoulder. Crouch, and peek around the doorway, noting the position of any occupants or sentries. The lower this is done the more effectively hidden you will be, since most people tend to look and search at eye level first. Key your actions to the movement of the enemy head by directing your attention to the base of his skull.

FIG. 52—Withdraw the head, maintaining a slight body pressure against the wall. As quickly and silently as possible, push off with the rear leg (the right in this case), stepping clear across the door opening in one swift motion. This will look like a quick sideways hop, landing on the left leg first. As you cross by this method, glance at the enemy by turning to look over your right shoulder. This is the safest way to pass an open doorway.

FIG. 53—Having gained a position on the opposite side of the doorway, assume the illustrated position and check around the corner to insure that your movement was not observed.

If one is confronted by an open doorway at night, with light falling across the path, it is preferable to move outside the circle of light, remaining invisible in the shadows.

MI LU PU (LOST TRACK PIVOT)

The last of the Nine Steps is the *Mi Lu Pu,* or Lost Track Pivot. It consists of two 90-degree side steps, turning the body to face oppositely from its original position. It is taken from the Lost Track Form, an ancient *kata* (practice form). During Inpo, it is best employed to dart behind cover; in Tonpo, it may be used to suddenly turn and face the enemy, or to gain a position behind him.

FIG. 54—Assume the following posture to practice this form. Stand in a basic Horse Stance, knees slightly bent with toes pointing forward, the body lowered slightly, shoulders squared, eyes looking straight ahead.

FIG. 55—Pivot on the ball of the right foot while turning toward your right forward corner. Draw the left foot to the right ankle as you turn, and step out to the left. You will now be facing 90 degrees away from your original position. Keep the shoulders square and hold the head steady. Do not try to keep looking forward, as this will upset your balance.

FIG. 54

FIG. 55

FIG. 56

FIG. 56—The instant the left foot touches the ground, shift the weight to that side and execute a second 90-degree pivot, this time to your right rear corner, by drawing the right foot to the left ankle and stepping out 90 degrees to the right. You now face 180 degrees from your first position.

This is sometimes known as the Spinning Back Pivot, or the Box Step. When employing this technique to duck behind cover, it is not always possible to make exact angles on these pivots. Only practice will enable you to master this. The exercise helps develop the legs and balance. It should be practiced by turning five times to the right and five to the left.

MORE KUJI ASHI WAYS TO MOVE

FIG. 57–When ascending a stairway, keep as close as possible to the wall and climb using Heng Pu, the Cross Step. On stone steps, this will aid in concealing your position; on wooden stairs, this will prevent creaking since the stairs are most secure nearest the wall and are thus less likely to shift as weight is applied.

FIG. 58–It was said in ancient times that a Ninja cast no shadow. This applies equally to casting a reflection. Never pass a mirror openly. Even a tiny movement is reflected to every angle and an observer with his back to you will almost certainly catch the action. Treat mirrors as open windows, and cross outside their field of reflection.

FIG. 59–Beware also of where your shadow falls. The human silhouette is distinctive and easily recognizable. Even if you are out of view, your shadow may fall across the path of the enemy, revealing your position.

In all these things, it is essential that you observe the enemy without being observed by him. Only in this way can you succeed.

FIG. 57

FIG. 58

FIG. 59

This concludes the movements of the Kuji Ashi, by which it is possible to advance from one point of concealment to another without fear of discovery.

It cannot be stressed too highly that silence and careful consideration are the keys to this phase of Ninjitsu.

5 Climbing Devices

The Ninja who is a skillful intelligence gatherer will know whether any special apparatus is necessary for the mission. Remember that any device may become an encumbrance.

NINJA-TO (SWORD OF DARKNESS)

Since the Ninja considered the utilitarian purpose of a device to be its most important value, it is little wonder that they devised new uses and variations for the traditional weapon of the warrior—the sword. One variation was the Ninja's emphasis on the straight thrust in combat, as opposed to the cut which was more classical.

Bear in mind that the *Ninja-To,* the Sword of Darkness, is considerably shorter than the traditional samurai blade. This contributed to specialization; close-combat swordplay as well as the techniques of *Iaijitsu,* or fast drawing methods, were thus emphasized.

The Ninja also considered the uses of the *tsubo* (fingerguard) and the scabbard. Even the parts of the blade were named and correlated to various functions. For example, the spine of the blade represented the concept of the shield, being the section which deflected or stopped the enemy attack; the flat of the blade was considered armor, and was the basis for the use of metal bars sewn into the sleeves of the Ninja costume for blocking, as well as the light chain mail which was occasionally worn; the edge of the blade, naturally, headed the category of *shaken,* weapons which are thrown or launched at the enemy (shurikens, arrows, etc.).

The tsubo, or fingerguard, of the Ninja-To was often larger than that of the samurai sword. Most often it was also square, as opposed to the traditional circular design. By virtue of these modifications, its value as a tool was enhanced.

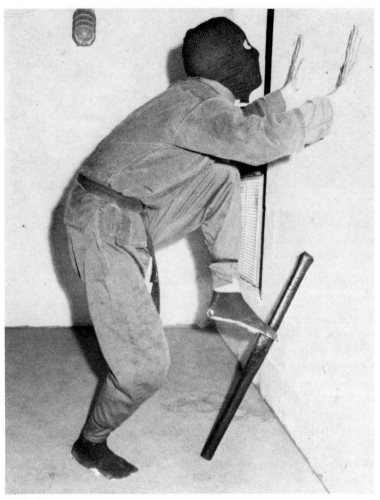

FIG. 60

FIG. 60—Best known of the uses was the practice of propping the sword against a wall and using the tsubo as a short step. The sword would then be drawn up by means of a cord attached to the scabbard. This method is seldom effective on walls over ten feet in height, but is quite useful for reaching the eaves of a house and gaining the roof.

FIG. 61

FIG. 61—A second purpose to which the tsubo could be put, in addition to a foothold, is that of a handhold. By hooking the tsubo over the lip of a low wall, sufficient purchase can be gained to pull oneself to the summit. Further, and this is by far the most suitable use, one can hang by this method when descending. Thus one can get closer to the ground and make less noise when dropping down.

CH'IANG PI CHU (WALL CLIMBING DEVICES)

The Ninja used a multitude of hooks, rakes, and collapsible ladders to scale enemy walls when necessary.

The grappling hook is by far the best auxiliary tool/weapon for the individual. It is small, easily concealable, light and, in the proper hands, noiseless. Further, the vicious hook can be used to flail the enemy, to entangle his weapon, or simply to beat him; the *sageo* (cord) can be employed as a whip, as a net, or to bind and strangle the enemy. The primary use, however, is in extending the reach of the user.

Hooks may be single, double, or multipointed. In an emergency the *sayo* (scabbard) can be tied at the end of the cord and wedged in a manner which will anchor the line.

The cord of the grapple is derived from sageo which the Ninja wore on his scabbard. The hook is a derivative of the tsubo.

It is advisable to attach a short length of chain between the hook and the cord to prevent fraying. This adds but little weight and actually increases the accuracy of the cast.

FIG. 62—Illustrated is the basic four-prong snatch-hook apparatus. The grapple consists of four steel hooks welded at right angles, ending in two rings; covered with approximately two ounces of lead (for weight). These may be purchased at any fishing supply house at reasonable cost, and of a size and nature to suit the user. The grapple is attached to the cord by means of a short length of chain, which is linked to the double rings in the ends of the grapple and to a loop in the end of the line by master links. The cord itself is nylon line, one-half inch in diameter. All of the above apparatus is capable of supporting at least 200 pounds. All scaling apparatus must be checked before use to insure safety.

The grapple and chain are normally held in the right hand, while the left holds the line loosely coiled.

Naturally, for the grappling hook to be effective, the implement itself must sail over the obstacle, and carry the cord with it. Then the hook may be set and the wall ascended. However, two things make this difficult: the method of casting the hook; and the play-out of the line. One can throw the grapple precisely into place, but if the line tangles or hangs up, the toss is useless.

Therefore, learn to coil the line.

FIG. 63—Hold approximately six inches of the cord between the ball of the thumb and the first joint of the index finger of the left hand. Take a similar grip about two feet down the cord with the right hand, and pull the line taut.

FIG. 64—Bring the right hand to the left, twisting the rope between the fingers of the right hand to impart a slight curl to the line. Slip this coil between the fingers of the left hand, forming a loop about eight inches in diameter in the left hand.

FIG. 65—Holding the loop in the left hand, slide the right hand down the rope the same distance as before, and coil another loop into the left hand, remembering to twist the line, until the entire twenty or so feet have been collected lariat-style in the left hand.

FIG. 62

FIG. 63

FIG. 64

FIG. 65

SPIN METHOD OF THROWING THE GRAPPLE

FIG. 66—Hold the grapple by the end of the chain and whirl it clockwise to build up momentum; the faster the spin, the higher the hook will sail. Centripetal force will cause the hook to fly off tangentially to the circular path which you are creating. Hold the rope loosely coiled in the left hand. Be careful to hold the hook away from the body, lest you accidentally hook your leg.

FIG. 67—Release the chain and grapple in an underhand toss in such a manner that the hook sails over the wall. Note that the line plays out of the left hand smoothly as the fingers are slightly opened.

This method is employed when it is necessary to scale an unusually high wall, or where there is little room to throw effectively.

FIG. 66   FIG. 67

HOOK METHOD OF THROWING THE GRAPPLE

FIG. 68—Hold the chain and grapple in the right hand by the loop. Let the grapple almost touch the ground near the right foot. Shift the weight slightly to the rear. Hold the rope loosely coiled in the left hand. Look at the spot where you want the grapple to strike.

FIG. 68 **FIG. 69** **FIG. 70**

FIG. 69—Sling the grapple over the wall in the same way you would shoot a hook shot in basketball. This is by far the most accurate method for scaling walls of moderate height. Note that the weight is shifted forward on the cast, and that the line feeds smoothly out of the coils in the left hand.

TOSS METHOD OF THROWING THE GRAPPLE

FIG. 70—Hold the grapple, chain and all, in the right hand. Hold the rope loosely coiled in the left hand. Toss the grapple upward over the wall, allowing the chain to play out en masse. This technique is used to place the grapple on the summit of a low wall.

CH'IANG SHENG KUNG (ROPE CLIMBING ABILITY)

Once the grapple has cleared the wall, the line is gradually pulled until the hook is set. This means that the hook digs into wood or stone sufficiently to hold your weight, or that the grapple becomes wedged between two obstructions tightly enough to hold you. Test the set by jerking sharply on the line to see if the hook is only snagged. If it is, this action will either dig the hook in, or pop the hook free.

Having set the hook, look about to see if your actions were observed. Then ascend.

FIG. 71—The quickest method for this is hand-over-hand with the ir feet braced against the wall. Gravity will hold your feet to the surface as you climb by alternately advancing the opposite arm and leg.

FIG. 72—In those cases where such wall walking is impractical, one may simply climb the rope. Some Ninja used a method of climbing which employed the toes to grip the rope. Since they wore the tabi (split-toed socks), this was a matter of toe strength in most cases. This can be accomplished, however, by tying knots at regular intervals, and stepping on them with the toes. Alternately, one can cross the legs and grip the rope between them to gain a bit more purchase for climbing.

FIG. 71   FIG. 72

FIG. 73—A third technique which may be used is the *seat method*. In this, the rope is slung under the body to form a loop where one can sit. The free end is held in the right hand, which holds the loop firm while the left hand advances on the rope. Next the right hand slides up to the left, adjusting the loop as the feet advance.

FIG. 73

By reversing this procedure, it is possible to lower oneself slowly over long distances. It might be said that this is a Ninjitsu type of rappelling.

FIG. 74—Once you reach the summit of the wall, immediately retrieve the rope and clear all evidence of your passage. If the rope is to be used for the Tonpo phase of the mission, conceal it where the crossing will be made. The hook is a disposable weapon, as is the shuriken. It can be left behind or discarded at any time. Still, it should not be left in such a way that it will betray your presence.

Remember also to avoid silhouetting while on top of the wall.

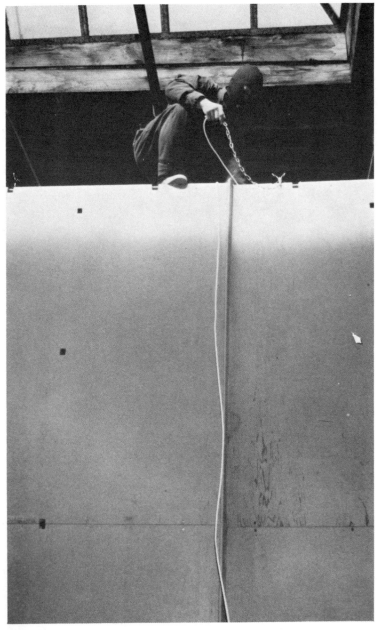

FIG. 74

6 Positions Of Concealment

Once the perimeter has been penetrated, one becomes concerned with invisibility inside the camp. There are six basic positions which may be used to conceal your presence.

FIGS. 75-78—A position *above* the enemy is the first of these. As has been mentioned, most people look at the horizon or scan their surroundings at eye level. The Ninja uses this propensity to his advantage. Approaching the point of penetration across the rooftops is fairly safe so long as one keeps low to avoid silhouetting. Further, one can flatten out on the roof and observe the enemy camp.

There is an ancient legend of a Ninja who entered an enemy camp and penetrated the attic of the enemy general. The Ninja drilled a tiny hole in the ceiling of the general's bedroom, lowered a thread through the opening, and dripped poison into the general's mouth as he slept. Attics are also excellent places to eavesdrop. Care must be taken to support one's weight only on the rafters, since many ceilings cannot support a person's weight.

FIGS. 79 & 80—One can also hide *below* the enemy when wishing to gather intelligence by eavesdropping. Examine dwellings for crawl spaces, air conditioning ducts, or cellars. Enter where you will not be seen and move using the She Pu (Serpent Step) beneath the floor to a spot where the enemy can be overheard. Remember to cover the penetration by replacing any trap doors or grates which may have barred your path.

Beware of being trapped above or below the enemy. When fleeing, never run to a position which will enable the enemy to tree you by sur-

FIG. 75

FIG. 76   **FIG. 77**   **FIG. 78**

FIG. 79

FIG. 80

FIG. 81

FIG. 82

FIG. 83

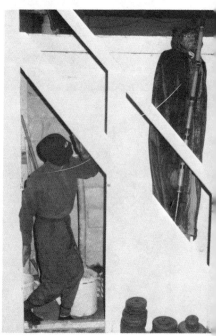

FIG. 84

rounding your higher position. When beneath the enemy, remember the tale of the Ninja who was speared through the floor by an alert guard when he noted an excessive amount of mosquito activity over the imprudent Ninja's hidden position.

FIGS. 81-84—*Beside* cover is a third method which may be used. Regardless of the object which you will employ, keep as low as possible. Look around cover to see the enemy. In this way you will be concealed partially by the object's shadow. When high visibility by the enemy makes it necessary to actually be beside an object, select the side on which the deepest shadow lies and conceal yourself within it, assuming the same shape.

FIG. 85—Hiding *behind* cover is the fourth technique. In selecting this approach, bear in mind that you must assume the shape of the object. That is, you must not allow any part of your body to show and reveal your position. Shrubs, hedges, crates, stacked materiel, and so on, may be used for this purpose.

FIG. 85

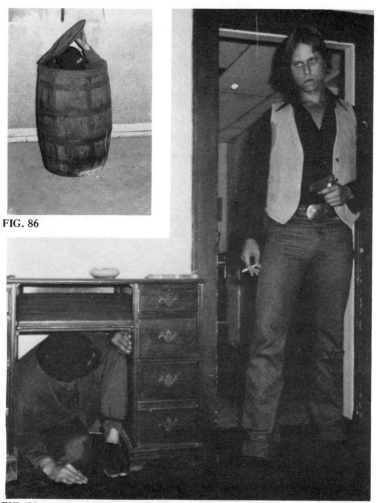

FIG. 86

FIG. 87

FIGS. 86 & 87—Hiding *inside* is another technique of conceal-ment. The trick is to choose places a person is not expected to fit. The Ninja must possess great flexibility and the ability to remain utterly still.

FIGS. 88 & 89—Hiding in *front* of cover is the boldest and most difficult of these concealment methods. To accomplish this, one must select the object of concealment, position himself directly before it, and assume its same shape. Lower the torso and slightly tense the Hara. Look directly ahead without fixing the eyes on any one point. Relax the body.

FIG. 88

In all of these concealment methods, the primary consideration is *no movement*. It is of utmost importance in *Joei-on no-jitsu,* or "hiding in plain view." This technique was a favorite of the ancient Ninja, who would position themselves so along a path traveled by the enemy, stepping forward to attack him as he passed. Do not look directly at the enemy; this will cause him to sense your presence.

FIG. 89

7 Covert Entry

Studies have shown that eight out of ten burglars enter through door-ways. This may be a matter of habit or personal taste. Certainly, door-ways are the most convenient means of ingress, but do not be limited to these.

Door latches may be jimmied or picked; each method has its advantages and its drawbacks. Hinge pins sometimes can be removed to allow entry, or panels can be cut out of the door itself. Always listen at the doorjamb for any sound of movement from within before opening a door. Upon entering, take a position behind the door and listen for sounds of discovery or pursuit.

Windows are the second easiest means of covert entry. Glass can be cut or pulled out of its frame. It can be broken out by taping in a crisscross manner and then covering the point of impact with a coat or jacket to muffle the sound. When employing this approach, be sure to remove and conceal any jagged bits of glass from the frame. A window frame with no glass will pass a cursory inspection, appearing to be a clear pane.

Air shafts can be used, but they generally have screens and filters which impede movement. Cellars and crawl spaces can be employed, though it may be necessary to cut through the floor. And further, they do not make for quick escapes.

Some methods, such as tunneling or breaking out a wall, are considered too tedious for true surreptitious entry.

FIG. 90

JU CH'UANG (ENTERING WINDOW)

Ju Ch'uang is a Ninjitsu technique concerned with entering by a window. Standing beside the wall side of the window, after compromising the latch or having determined that it is unlatched, open the aperture.

FIG. 90—Grip the top and bottom of the opening if possible; if not, grip both sides. Pull the body forward, extending one leg into the room. Shift weight forward, projecting yourself inside. Place both hands inside, pushing yourself over the lead leg. Draw the trailing leg inside. Crouch beside the window, then close it behind you. Remain motionless for a few seconds and listen for any indication that your passage was observed.

Second-story windows and those which open onto unoccupied rooms are preferred.

SO HAO TSUI (LOCK-PICKING FORM)

When confronted by a locked door, recourse sometimes must be made to the art of *So Hao Tsui,* or Lock-Picking Form. The ancient Ninja developed special tools for slipping the latches of their enemies.

FIG. 91—To employ such tools, one kneels at the door, adjusting height so that eyes are even with the lock. In the case of modern manipulation, the turning wrench is held in the left hand, applied with a slight pressure, while the pick is inserted and used to set the pin tumblers by the right.

This posture is preferable especially at night, since it offers some concealment. There is a method known as *raking,* in which the pick is used in a rapid to-and-fro action to bounce the tumblers free. While raking, one should stand and appear to be trying to make a proper key work. This technique is often used by hotel burglars. If they are discovered, they can pretend to be closing the door instead of opening it.

NING SHIH LIEN (PEEKING THROUGH THE CRACK)

FIG. 92—When encountering a door which is slightly ajar, approach the hinge side of the threshold, reach across the door, and lightly grasp the latch. Scan the interior of the room beyond by looking through the crack between the doorjamb and the door itself. You may slowly open or close the door to allow more of the interior to come into view, bearing in mind that extremely slow movement is not visible.

Never stand in front of a door even if it is closed, since doors are easily penetrated by gunfire. Police use a variation of this position when preparing to enter a room occupied by armed suspects.

FIG. 91 **FIG. 92**

JU MEN (ENTERING DOOR)

FIG. 93—When confronted by a closed door, approach its latch side. Press your back to the wall next to the jamb. Slowly open the latch using the right hand and peek inside through the aperture thus provided. Place the left hand on the wall near the shoulder and be prepared to push off and escape should you draw attention.

In all instances, listening at the doorjamb is equally as important as trying to see inside.

Ju Men Pu, sixth step of the Kuji Ashi, is used to enter a doorway without being observed. At night, when you enter a lighted room, light will escape as the door is opened, revealing your presence. If the interior is unlit, the shadow cast by the door, or its very movement may give you away.

FIG. 94—To overcome this, press the shoulder against the doorjamb, gripping the latch with the left hand. Open the door quietly, inch by inch, and move slowly forward. Hold the cloak or hand above the head, lightly touching the top of the door, to fill the newly formed opening.

FIG. 95—Press into the opening, filling the gap and allowing no light to escape. Step in and back with the right foot first. Slide the hips in, then the shoulders. The head, the left foot, and lastly the right hand are drawn inside. The right hand is lowered only after the door is closed from within.

FIG. 93

FIG. 94

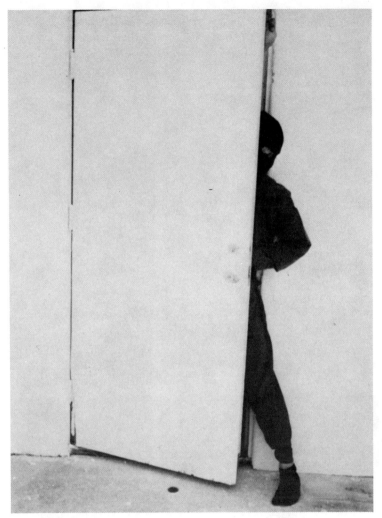

FIG. 95

By this method, the door is opened only slightly, lessening the chance that the hinges will creak, or that the movement of the door will betray you.

LI TSU AN (HIDING IN THE DOOR'S SHADOW)

Inside, if you hear the approach of a sentry, dart to a position behind the door where you may utilize *Li Tsu An,* or Hiding in the Door's Shadow. The sentry may pass outside without entering. The sentry may open the door and look inside without entering.

FIG. 96

FIG. 96—Here you can see the sentry through the crack in the doorjamb. He may be suspicious and enter. In this event you will be blocked from view by the door. Or the sentry may enter and search. Should this occur, remember that if the door is opened at least ninety degrees, sufficient shadow will be cast to conceal you. If the door is opened farther, you will remain hidden behind it.

The most difficult time occurs when the sentry has entered and searched, and is preparing to leave. As he nears the door he will be looking directly at you. At this time great courage is required not to move and betray your position. The odds are that the sentry will be at ease, having found no one in the room; he may drop his guard or lower his weapon as an indication of this. He will be thinking of his exit, possibly berating himself for his suspicions. Watch his eyes; if they are downcast, he will not see you. If the light switch is near the door, he may shift his gaze to it as he nears you, and this will insure your invisibility.

If he sees you, you must spring upon him and silence him instantly. One school advocates whipping around the door, slamming it and locking the sentry in behind you if discovered. But this is not true Ninjitsu.

KEN SUI SHAO PING
(FOLLOWING IN THE FOOTSTEPS OF THE SENTRY)

FIG. 97—Having advanced to a position behind the enemy, fix your attention on the back of his skull and key your actions to his. As he steps forward with his left foot, cross-step (Heng Pu) behind with your right foot. Cock your left backfist beside the right ear. Maintain a covered stance at all times by crossing the right arm over the body. Direct the Chi forward with the right palm.

You can strike the enemy sentry at any time when following him in this manner (*Ken Sui Shao Ping*) by whipping out with the left backfist, opening the hand at the moment of impact to strike the base of his skull in an upward stroke with the sword edge of the hand (*Shuto*). The impact of this blow must be sufficient to lift the skull free of the cervical vertebrae and sever the spinal cord. Death is instantaneous.

Continue to follow the sentry by this sequence.

FIG. 98—As the enemy steps forward with his right foot, step out with your left. This places you in a karate frontal stance, with your left side to the enemy. The arms remain as before; the left fist is tensed and will act as *Mu-Te* or Striking Hand, while the right hand shields the

FIG. 97

FIG. 98

body. These steps must be executed quickly and lightly; they also must be synchronized with the enemy's steps so that he does not hear you.

FIG. 99—The enemy has advanced to his objective. Cross-step behind once more, adjusting balance to keep your shape behind the enemy's shoulders. When following in this manner, it does not matter if the enemy should sense your presence and quickly move around to catch you. This is due to the time lag factor between seeing, identifying, and acting.

It does not matter in which stance he may catch you, and it does not matter which way he turns, though most often he will pivot forward (to his left rear if his right foot is forward).

In certain cases it may be necessary to follow a sentry in order to pass through locked doors. Once the door is open, shift body weight forward and turn his corner, bringing yourself into his peripheral view. This will cause him to turn toward you.

FIG. 100—Jam his right arm since it holds the weapon, and simultaneously strike into his face with the left backfist. Here the right hand acts as *Soe-Te,* or Entangling Hand. Strike his nose directly as this will cause uncontrollable watering of the eyes, as well as muffle any outcry. This allows you sufficient time to permanently quiet him.

FIG. 99   **FIG. 100**

8 Sentry Removal

It may be necessary to eliminate a sentry in order to penetrate the enemy camp. The principle of *Nyudaki No Jitsu* is used to take advantage of the psychological weakness of a sentry. *Nyudaki* is translated from the Japanese to mean "idleness" or a "dislike for being industrious." It is advisable to select your target carefully. Bear three things in mind when seeking to discover the shortcomings of an enemy: first, never look down on the enemy and underestimate him; second, never fear the enemy and act without confidence; and third, never hesitate.

In attacking a sentry, two facets should be considered: he must be killed as quickly as possible, and he must make no outcry. It is preferable to remove a sentry when he will be least missed, such as shortly after post checks that occur at regular intervals.

People sleep most deeply between 3:00 and 5:00 A.M. The body is accustomed to this cycle. Therefore, a sentry, nearing the end of the watch, shortly after a post check, and just before dawn, is a prime target. He probably will not be missed until the changing of the guard. Also, those inside the camp will be in their deepest sleep and thus are less likely to hear a muffled cry.

FIG. 101—Approach to within three or four feet of the enemy and assume the illustrated stance. This will enable you to make a lightning strike by springing on him. The dagger is held in the lead hand (*Mu-Te*) while the left arm acts to seize and hold the enemy for the knife thrust (*Soe-Te*).

FIG. 101   **FIG. 102**

Discussed next are the five assassination options open to the knife-wielding Ninja: *Slitting the Throat; Kidney Thrust; Subclavian Artery Thrust; Jugular Thrust;* and the *Heart Thrust.*

SLITTING THE THROAT

FIG. 102—Spring forward and cup the enemy chin with the left palm, lifting it clear of the throat. Draw the blade across the throat at the level of the cricoid cartilage, beginning at the hilt and stroking to the tip. This attack slices the trachea, preventing any sort of outcry; then cuts deeper, severing the carotid sheath. The sentry dies in twelve seconds due to oxygen starvation of the brain. Unconsciousness occurs in five seconds.

KIDNEY THRUST

FIG. 103—Spring forward, whipping the left wrist into the enemy's trachea to prevent outcry. The effectiveness of this blow is easily demonstrated by tapping one's Adam's apple with only one-twentieth of the force required. This action disrupts the phrenic nerve, causing the diaphragm to cease pumping air in and out of the lungs. Simultaneously drive the dagger into the kidney horizontally. Cut to both sides by

FIG. 103   FIG. 104

pushing and pulling the wrist side to side. Death results in thirty seconds and no help of man can prevent it.

SUBCLAVIAN ARTERY THRUST

FIG. 104—Spring forward and clamp the left hand over the enemy mouth and nose in the method known as the One-Hand Smother. Pulling the nose between your thumb and the first joint of the opposing index finger. Grip the jaws between the heel of the hand and the remaining finger tips. This method alone will require almost two minutes to produce unconsciousness. Holding the dagger in the ice-pick grip, thrust the point well down behind the collarbone (clavicle) and cut side to side. Death will result in three seconds from severing the subclavian artery.

JUGULAR THRUST

FIG. 105—Spring forward and employ the One-Hand Smother. Pull the enemy's head to the left and thrust the dagger with edges parallel to the ground well into the leading edge of the sterno-cleio-mastoideus muscle running around the side of the neck. This severs the carotid sheath which contains the carotid artery, jugular vein, and vagus nerve.

FIG. 105   FIG. 106

Cut side to side. Death ensues in twelve seconds, unconsciousness in five.

HEART THRUST

FIG. 106—Spring forward, sliding your left arm over the enemy right arm and up to clamp over his mouth from below. Bend him backwards, breaking his balance to the rear. Drive the knife slightly upward under the rib cage, into the chest cavity to penetrate the heart. Cut side to side. Death comes in three seconds, unconsciousness is induced instantly.

Very likely these attacks will cause the enemy to drop his weapon, or knock off his helmet or headgear. Should this occur, make no attempt to prevent these incidental noises. Remain still for about ten seconds, listen for sounds of pursuit. It is probable that slight noises will be overlooked, especially if they are unrecognizable. Hearing no sound of pursuit, use the hold of your left arm to drag or carry the sentry backward out of sight.

In selecting a knife, three factors should be considered: durability, keenness, and balance. The handle should fit comfortably in the hand. It is essential that the blade have a sharp stabbing point and clean cutting edges. An artery which is torn through by a dull blade tends to contract. An artery which is cleanly severed bleeds freely and is usually a fatal wound.

9 Attacking From Ambush

Classical Ninjitsu states that there are three basic methods of attacking a sentry from ambush: from above, below, and behind. The initial attack must always be totally incapacitating, while catching the enemy off-guard.

AMBUSH FROM ABOVE

FIG. 107—Begin by gaining a position above the enemy using the Kuji Ashi, or hide in a superior position and wait for the enemy to come into range. Bear in mind that when being attacked from above, people seldom look up, and they tend to shoot under the target when firing up. Fix your gaze on the back of the enemy skull.

FIG. 108—Drop on the enemy, striking him with your full weight. Employ the knees to strike his shoulders and drive him straight down, breaking your own fall with his body. Try not to land directly on his head; though this frequently snaps the neck, the body does not fall properly. Should the enemy hear or sense your attack as you launch it and turn about, the attack will still succeed.

FIG. 109—Ride the enemy body to the ground, crushing his spine beneath you. Apply the coup de grace by striking the base of the skull with the right Shuto, breaking the neck.

AMBUSH FROM BELOW

When cover is scarce or low, consider attacking from below. Select a point of concealment above which the enemy will pass and from which you may launch your assault unseen.

FIG. 107

FIG. 108

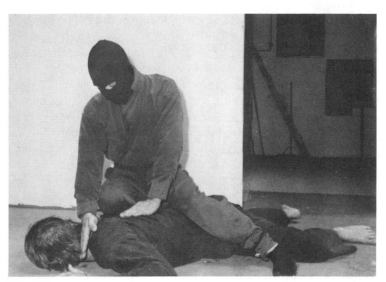

FIG. 109

FIG. 110—As the enemy passes, cup his rear foot in the palm of your hand (the right in this case), simultaneously poising the dagger in your left.

FIG. 111—Scoop the enemy foot forward as he shifts his weight forward onto his lead foot, lifting it clear of the ground and breaking his balance to the rear. Cock the dagger beside your left ear in an ice-pick grip.

FIG. 112—As the enemy falls beside you, landing on his shoulders, pivot over your right knee and drive the dagger downward into his heart. It is essential that you sweep the enemy as he takes his weight off his rear foot. This prevents him from saving himself by taking a quick step forward.

AMBUSH FROM BEHIND

Advance to a position behind the enemy, armed in this case with a garrote. This consists of a length of thin steel cable approximately two feet long.

110   FIG. 111

FIG. 112

FIG. 113—Wrap the ends of the cable around your fists and grip the central position with the thumbs. Some schools advocate crossing the garrote, forming a loop to slip over the enemy head. This merely makes the attack more difficult and less likely to succeed.

FIG. 114—Drop the garrote over the enemy's head and pull back with both hands, exerting sufficient pressure to force the enemy backward. His reaction will be to try to seize the garrote and relieve the pressure against his throat. This attack affects the trachea, preventing any outcry, as well as shutting off the blood supply to the brain through the carotid artery.

FIG. 115—Continue to exert choking pressure with the arms, crossing the fists behind the enemy neck. Drive the knee upward into the small of his back, breaking the spine. To finish him off, you can twist to your right, dropping him face down, and sit atop him on your knee until he ceases to struggle.

FIG. 113   FIG. 114   FIG. 115

SHIMEWAZA (JAPANESE STRANGLE)

Any time you are behind the enemy you may seek to employ the Japanese Strangle to subdue him. This technique may be applied while standing, sitting (as after a throw), or on the mat. Three variations are possible.

The *Rear Naked Choke* is not a true strangle hold, but one in which the pressure of the forearm is directed against the windpipe. This hold is quite painful, causing the enemy to struggle more violently. This choke, however, will induce unconsciousness, usually when the strangle is improperly applied.

FIG. 116—In the *Classical Method,* whip the left forearm around the enemy throat, striking him on the trachea with the inside edge of the wrist or hand. This action will cause him to inhale sharply. Continue the action until the crook of the left forearm/elbow lies against the injured trachea. The left bicep will press against the left side of the enemy neck, while the left forearm will press against the right. Clamp the right palm behind the enemy skull with the finger tips behind his left ear. This will be used to push him forward into the left elbow.

FIG. 117—Grip your right bicep with your left palm. Relax the left arm and push with the right palm. This is not a punishing hold to the enemy, since he could still breath if your throat-strike had not damaged the phrenic nerve. Pressure is directed instead to the sides of the neck,

FIG. 116   FIG. 117

specifically against the carotid artery which collapses in a ribbonlike manner when one inhales. When the supply of blood to the brain is cut off, unconsciousness results in five seconds. If the hold is improperly applied and only one artery is sealed, unconsciousness will begin in ten to fifteen seconds.

It is possible to revive a person rendered unconscious by this technique, but this is employed in sport applications only.

The *Tel Shia Technique* is useful should the enemy seek to escape by reaching behind to strike your groin. Extend the fingers of both hands forming the Shuto with each, then step quickly back with the right leg and pull him down. This action will dislocate the skull from the spinal column resulting in instant death.

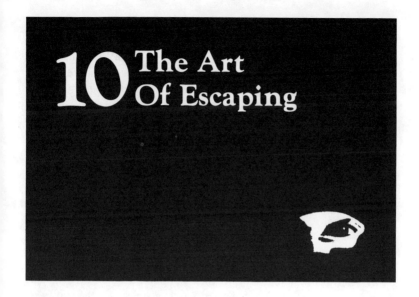

10 The Art Of Escaping

Tonpo, the Art of Escaping, may be divided into three phases. The *hideout* may be a point of concealment inside the enemy camp or on its perimeter. It is a temporary refuge only. The *refuge* refers to a hiding place within enemy control but sufficiently safe to allow rest or regrouping. The refuge may be known to an indigenous ally or take the form of a disguise. The FBI and CIA frequently use this device. They are known as safe houses and new identities. The *sanctuary* consists of a position outside the control of enemy forces, where friendly forces can assist you. Beware of these situations, however; even here, a Ninja is not truly safe.

Previously stressed has been the importance of observing the enemy, his encampment, and so on. For the most part, the escape route should be the same as the penetration route. It should be retraced stealthily, as if one were entering instead of leaving; indeed, this is penetration outwards. The reason for using the same route is that less likelihood exists of being discovered. Also, since the route has been used once, it is more familiar. Great care must be taken not to let one's guard down during Tonpo.

No one can plan for all contingencies, but one can try. To this end, at least two other escape routes should be available, one directly opposite and the other veering ninety degrees from the original path. These are to be employed in the event of the primary route's discovery.

In selecting the primary route, look for means to employ stealth. In selecting alternatives, look first for means to employ speed and cover. Second, look for areas where distractions can be created. If possible, locate and prepare an escape route from the guardhouse for use in the unlikely event you are captured. Bear in mind that when being pursued, it may be necessary to stand and fight. Select points along the escape route that have the advantage of high ground, and note that doorways and gates can often be held by one man. In short, any spot where the enemy will be hampered by obstacles can be used to the escaping Ninja's advantage.

Avoid inhabited areas such as barracks, mess halls, or command posts. Beware of booby traps, mined or alarmed areas, and those brightly lit. The location and strength of every guard post should be known before entering.

Long-term escape and evasion may include identity changes and familiarization with public and private means of transportation, border patrols, and security checks. Numerous works exist on these subjects*, which are not directly connected with pure Ninjitsu.

However, in modern warfare, these considerations must be planned for assiduously. Nothing can be left to chance because the stakes are life and death.

P'ENG WEI (CRASHING OUT)

The first principle of Tonpo is to escape as quickly as possible. The longer you remain in enemy control, the less likely you are to escape. Should your presence be discovered, vanish and follow your escape route to freedom. Should you be captured, and it becomes necessary to attempt escape from a guardhouse, consider the *P'eng Wei*, or Crash Out.

FIG. 118—Locked doors which open outward may be kicked open in P'eng Wei, using the Dragon Stamp Kick or the more common Side Kick. Direct the force of the blow as close to the latch as possible, the object being to shatter the doorjamb with the bolt.

FIG. 119—The shoulder also can be used to force open the door. When striking the door with the shoulder, apply the force as near the center of the door as possible. This will bend the door, pulling the lock bolt clear of the doorjamb to spring it open. Doors with panels will shatter, causing you to fall forward. It is necessary that you roll out to avoid losing momentum. Striking with the shoulder may also be used against flimsy doors which open inward.

---

*Paladin Press publishes numerous books on identity changing, escape and evasion, intelligence gathering, and espionage. Write to P.O. Box 1307, Boulder, Colorado 80306, for a complete catalog of Paladin Press titles.

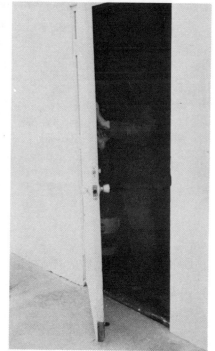

FIG. 118   FIG. 119

To accomplish this feat requires a running start from several feet away. This adds momentum and impact.

A third P'eng Wei possibility calls for diving out a window. Again, it is essential to execute a forward roll on impact to avoid injury and to maintain momentum. In the case of diving out, you will land on the hands, which must collapse, allowing the shoulders to bear the brunt of the fall.

Diving through glass is not recommended, though it may be necessary if the window's lock cannot be compromised. In this event, cross both arms over the head to protect the face and eyes and drive forward. Extend the arms to break your fall once clear of the window, not before. Diving through glass with the arms extended results in serious injuries.

Sufficient forward momentum must be generated to clear the windowsill, since jagged bits of glass will cling to the frame and slash you. Never dive through a large plate glass window or door. Glass from the upper portion will fall and spear you before you can get clear. Smash these large windows with a chair or similar object, then escape.

LAO TSU CHI HUO (DROP TOE HOLD)

The following is an escape to be employed when the Ninja is detained in the military frisk position.

FIG. 120—Note that the enemy hooks your leg with his left leg to sweep your feet from under you should you resist. His left hand presses against your back, locking the vertebrae and forcing him to raise the pistol over his arm.

FIG. 121—As pressure is applied to your back, tuck your arms and fall straight forward, twisting to your left rear. Break this fall by seizing the enemy's right wrist, pulling him forward and turning the weapon to the outside. Land on your left hip, driving your left knee behind his left knee. Catch his left ankle with the crotch of your right knee. Drive your right palm upward into his hip, striking his left hip socket. Watch the pistol. He may resist, trying to keep his balance, or spasmodically get off a shot.

FIG. 122—Pull down and push up with your hands. Swing the body to the right, using your weight to slam the enemy into the wall. Slip your leg between the enemy legs and scissor his left leg with your own. This trips him forward and prevents him from saving himself. This movement must be executed with blinding speed.

FIG. 120

FIG. 121

FIG. 122

SHOU K'AO K'AI (HANDCUFF SWITCH)

The enemy has captured you and ordered your hands atop your head. He moves into position behind you and reaches up to take your right arm into a hammer lock. This is preparatory to tying your hands or handcuffing them behind your back. The enemy presses his weapon into your back to discourage resistance. In an arrest, one officer generally covers the other.

FIG. 123—The enemy pulls your arm behind your back. This is the best moment to attack since he must either reach for his cuffs or holster his weapon. His attention will be distracted.

FIG. 124—Step to the right with your left foot, pivoting on the ball of the right foot, and reversing the enemy's wristlock by lifting it

FIG. 123   FIG. 124   FIG. 125

over your head and seizing his arm. Slap the enemy weapon to the outside with the left hand by crossing the body. This is known as a cross-
push block. If he has holstered his weapon, strike him in the rib cage as
you turn.

FIG. 125—Slide-step with the right foot to a position even with the
enemy. Step to his rear with your left foot, maintaining your grip on
his wrist. Pull downward in a semicircular arc with your right hand,
twisting the enemy's right arm into a hammer lock. Seize the enemy's
left wrist from behind to prevent his executing a similar reverse.

TEARING OFF THE FINGER

FIG. 126—This method is employed should the enemy be so fool-
ish as to place his weapon against your chest to intimidate you.

FIG. 127—Slap down with the right hand, clamping it over the
pistol. Two things are essential: the web of the hand must fall between
the hammer and the firing pin to prevent discharging a round; and the
weapon must be deflected down and to the left outside line, just in
case. In the case of revolvers, it is further possible to grip the cylinder
and keep it from turning. This prevents the weapon from firing.

FIG. 128—Having secured the grip, twist the barrel back upon
the enemy. This traps his finger inside the trigger guard. Seize his wrist
with your left hand to reinforce the finger lock. The enemy will most
likely seize your right elbow to resist this attack. In this event, step
quickly back with the right foot, jerking down on the weapon. The

FIG. 126   FIG. 127   FIG. 128

index finger will dislocate at the knuckle and can be torn off using the metal edges of the trigger guard.

ESCAPE BY TURNING

FIG. 129—Should the enemy apprehend you and place his weapon at your back, consider the point at which he actually touches you. This will determine the type of block you will employ when turning. In most instances, a mirror block will be most effective since, as you turn, your shoulder will drop. In this, as in the previous technique, be assured that it is possible to act before the enemy can fire. In both cases, your first concern is moving out of the line of fire, either by deflecting the weapon or by shifting your position.

FIG. 130—Pivot on the balls of both feet simultaneously. Execute a right mirror block to deflect the weapon to the outside line. Execute a left hooking arc with the left palm-heel, striking the enemy on the mastoid process. This consists of the small bony ridge just under the ear. Bear in mind that the carotid sheath is near the surface at this point also. The impact should be sufficient to dislocate the jaw.

By these means, the enemy can be disarmed.

ESCAPE FROM HEADLOCK

This technique works well against a rear naked choke or side head-lock. Should the enemy seize you and seek to employ the rear choke, the first consideration is freeing the windpipe.

FIG. 129   FIG. 130

FIG. 131—This is accomplished by turning toward the fist side of the choke and pinching down on the enemy wrist, attacking the ulnar or radial nerve depending on which side of the wrist is exposed. Pressure against this point will cause the enemy to release you slightly. Should you turn into his elbow, you will be helping him strangle you.

FIG. 132—By struggling with the enemy at his wrist, bend him slightly forward and back-out step with your right leg. As you do so, drop your right shoulder in such a way that you slip past his hip. The enemy will seek to maintain his hold by clinching down with his locked arms. This is to your advantage since it draws you to his hip, slipping you from the choke to a side headlock. Reach behind the enemy's left knee with your left hand. Reach up and over his shoulder to cup his chin with your right palm.

FIG. 133—Simultaneously pull with your right arm and lift with your left arm, taking the enemy off his feet. Step quickly back with your right foot a second time, dropping to your left knee in so doing. Pull the enemy backward and drop him over your right knee, snapping his spine.

FIG. 131

FIG. 132

FIG. 133

FIG. 134   FIG. 135

K'AI KUAN (STANDING SWITCH)

Should the enemy seize you about the waist in seeking to capture you, it is possible to reverse positions with him or escape by employing the Standing Switch.

FIG. 134—As the waist cinch is secured, drive your left arm down along the inside of the enemy's knee. This locks his elbow between your hip and tricep. Toe-out with the left foot and drop the left shoulder.

FIG. 135—Pivot on the ball of the left foot, swinging the right leg for added momentum. This action will certainly break the waist cinch or dislocate the enemy's elbow. Step behind the enemy with your right foot, maintaining a grip on his thigh with your left hand. From here you may step behind with the left foot and cinch him, or slide up and apply the Japanese Strangle.

LUN T'OU (WHEEL THROW)

FIG. 136—Should the enemy seize you by both wrists, free your hands by rotating them up and to the outside line. Step forward with the left foot, striking with double palm heels to the enemy's chest. This will drive him slightly back, braking his balance to the rear. Grip the

FIG. 136

FIG. 137

FIG. 138

FIG. 139

FIG. 140

enemy lapels with both hands. If lapels are not available, cup both hands behind his head.

FIG. 137—Maintaining your hold on the enemy, sit down near your left heel, pulling him forward and onto you, taking advantage of his natural reaction in trying to save himself from being pushed backward. Execute *Ke-Age* (kicking up) with the right leg. Strike the enemy groin or Hara.

FIG. 138—Use your grip on the enemy to support him over you. This prevents his falling forward too fast and striking you with his head. Place the left foot in the enemy's Hara and push up strongly with both legs, lifting him off the ground.

FIG. 139—Push the enemy clear allowing him to backfall to a head-to-head position above you. The impact alone of this fall is sufficient to drive the air from his lungs and incapacitate him. Using your grip on the enemy to maintain your momentum, execute a back roll swinging the feet overhead, tucking the head to one side, and pulling with both hands.

FIG. 140—Completing the back roll, land with the buttocks on the enemy chest or abdomen, driving the air from his lungs and crushing the chest cavity. Both knees should land on his biceps, rupturing the muscles. Release the grip on the enemy with the right hand and execute a driving palm heel to the enemy chin, snapping his neck.

ERH LUNG TE (TWIN DRAGON FIST)

These techniques are used in the event the enemy is successful in cornering you and launches a fist attack. They result in the enemy's permanent blindness, making possible your escape.

FIG. 141—Should the enemy throw a right lead, fall back slightly and counter with a right mirror-block. This action crosses the enemy with his own arm, preventing him from using his left hand to attack. Bear in mind that in Ninjitsu one does not truly block—one strikes. Therefore, the mirror-block is actually an attack to the wrist. By striking the ulnar nerve at this point, one numbs the arm.

FIG. 142—Immediately overturn with the right hand, trapping the enemy's right wrist and pulling him forward. Remember, he is forward already, heaving advanced to launch his attack in the first place. This action pulls him even farther, breaking his balance. As you begin to tip the enemy over, extend the left hand palm down, with the index and middle fingers outstretched. This forms the Twin Dragon Fist. The third and little fingers are curled into the hand. Do not stiffen the fingers as they will be easily broken. Do not drive forward with the fingers; rather, draw the enemy to them. No great amount of strength is required—only accuracy.

FIG. 141

FIG. 142

FIG. 143

FIG. 144

FIG. 143—If the enemy is more cautious and launches a left jab or hook, fall back slightly, executing a right shoulder-block. Again, you are actually attacking the wrist, in this case the radial nerve. This action opens the enemy center line to attack.

FIG. 144—Before the enemy's arm can be recovered from his left jab, strike out from the right shoulder-block position with the Twin Dragon Fist, attacking the eyes. Do not stiffen the fingers; imitate the action of a serpent striking. Use the left arm to execute a depressing forearm block as you lash out. This will deflect any attack that might have been launched by the enemy's right fist or, as in this case, will trap his left arm, preventing him from saving himself.

11 Nunchaku Techniques

As weapons masters, the Ninja naturally excelled in the way of the *Shuang Chin Kun,* or "double-close club." Known today as the *nunchaku,* the weapon consists of two short rods or sticks approximately as long as the user's forearm, connected by a length of cord as long as the width of the user's hand. Normally, one rod is held and the free rod is swung to strike the target. Naturally, the impact of the striking end is multiplied by the action of centrifugal force, making the device quite formidable.

Numerous books have been written concerning the uses of the nunchaku, and most *yudansha* (black belts) are familiar with it. Each ryu has its specialty: some employ the ends of the rods for striking by holding both sticks; others twist the cord around the wrists or neck of the enemy and apply crushing pressure with the rods; still others hold the rods in a straight line and use them like a *jo* (short staff). Basically, however, whipping the free end into the target is the preferred method.

The great advantage of the nunchaku is its ability to confuse the enemy. The user can release either end as he attacks, making it virtually impossible to predict from which angle the strike is coming; he may drive the enemy back by whipping the free rod in a figure-eight pattern between himself and the enemy; or he may strike out strongly, allow the free rod to swing around his body, reverse the action, and strike out again to the same line. The nunchaku generates as much as sixteen hundred foot-pounds of force at the point of impact and, since only eight pounds are required to break the bones of the arm, conventional blocks are useless. Further, the weapons are so destruc-

111

tive that even a poorly placed blow is extremely effective, and students are admonished to exercise caution when practicing lest they injure themselves.

The nunchaku was popularized through motion pictures. Bruce Lee slaying five or ten opponents, the sound of the hard wooden rods smashing bone and cartilage, and the dazzling display of *passes* (changing which end is free) with the rods almost whistling around his body mesmerized the martial arts audience. Yet until that time, the nunchaku was taught only to those who had reached the black belt level.

Still, the nunchaku is such a simple weapon that merely by having a pair and randomly experimenting, one can reach a stage of competence on a par with some experts.

In Ninjitsu, the Shuang Chin Kun is taught as an adjunct to the art of Tonpo. When surrounded and outnumbered, the Ninja would turn his nunchaku into whirling rods of death and fight his way to freedom.

BASIC STANCE

The basic fighting stance for the nunchaku is a variation of the *Shotokan Zenkutsu Dachi,* or "forward leaning stance."

FIG. 145—The shoulders are square to the enemy, the weight is distributed 60 per cent on the lead leg, 40 per cent on the rear leg. The weapon is gripped, one rod in each hand, with the cord taut. The arms are rounded, protecting the ribs. This stance is best used when launching an attack forward.

FIG. 145   **FIG. 146**

FIG. 147   FIG. 148

STRAIGHT THRUST

While the basic technique of the nunchaku has been described as swinging the free end to strike the target, Ninjitsu also teaches a method of striking directly forward without spinning the free rod. The striking surface of the blow is the butt of the stick.

FIG. 146—Begin with the free rod (*sakon*) trapped in the right armpit, and the right rod (*ukon*) gripped in the right fist. The left hand is held defensively in front of the body with the left hand protecting the face and the left elbow protecting the solar plexus.

FIG. 147—Pull strongly straight forward with the right hand jerking the sakon straight out to strike the target with the *kontei* (bottom of the rod). The action of the free rod is this: as it clears the arm, the top of the rod (*konto*) will move directly toward the target until it reaches the end of the cord (*sheng*), then it will stop. The bottom of the rod, by virtue of its greater mass and the momentum already gathered by the action of the right arm, will flip over, turning toward the target. This then will continue until the end of the cord is again reached (the cord will twist down and be pointing toward the user as the free rod flips). The kontei will thus pop the target, snapping back slightly.

FIG. 148—Rotate the wrist clockwise, swinging the sakon back toward the right armpit. The action of the sakon will describe a half-circle below the arm.

FIG. 149   **FIG. 150**

FIG. 149—As the sakon swings back under the arm striking the inside of the bicep, drop the right elbow down to the right hip and again trap the free end.

Practice this technique by attempting to snuff out a candle without hitting it. When you can do this you will have mastered the straight thrust.

The beauty of this movement is that the enemy, if he is familiar with nunchaku, will expect a circular, swinging attack. This short linear strike is so fast that the enemy will be caught off guard.

T'OU SHE (CAST).

Although the nunchaku is primarily a defensive weapon, there are offensive movements. The best of these is the Cast (*T'ou She*). Again, the kontei is the striking surface.

FIG. 150—Lay the rods one atop the other and slide the uppermost one back to the limit of the cord, offsetting the ends. Raise the rods to a position near the right ear, gripping both rods in one hand. Extend the left arm for balance.

Creep up behind the enemy making as little sound as possible.

FIG. 151

FIG. 151—Execute the Dart Throw described in the chapter on *Tonki-no-kata* (Nine Ways of Throwing), releasing the uppermost rod straight toward the target and retaining your grip on the lower rod with the right hand. The best target for this attack is the base of the skull.

Should it be necessary to use this technique while facing the enemy, aim for the center of the face. After the strike, the free rod may be retrieved by catching it with the fingers of the right hand.

DROP PASS

Reference has been made to *passing* the nunchaku. This usually involves holding one end of the weapon and swinging the other end around the body in such a manner that it may be caught by the other hand. In this way, the user can quickly switch his attack from one line

FIG. 152　　　　FIG. 153　　　　FIG. 154

to another, confusing the enemy as to his real intent. Passes also may be executed at the conclusion of a strike as the free end begins to lose momentum.

Ninjitsu has carried this portion of methodology one step further than most practitioners by devising several ways to vanish the weapon. These are sometimes known as invisible passes.

FIG. 152–The first of these is the *Ti Lao Kou,* or Drop Pass. Begin with the sakon trapped in the right armpit as shown, and the left hand in a defensive position in front of the body.

Open the right hand and lift the right elbow slightly away from the body while retaining your grip on the left rod with the armpit. Sufficient clearance must be provided between the elbow and the right hip to allow the ukon to swing between them, but the armpit must remain tight enough to hold the other end. This may take some practice, but is not as difficult as it may sound.

FIG. 153–As the sakon swings through the gap provided, momentum will carry it far enough behind the body so that the left hand, reaching around the small of the back, can catch it. Note that the left hand moves from its defensive position around the back *while* the ukon is swinging back to meet it. The timing on this is tricky, but not impossible.

FIG. 154–Grasping the sakon in the left hand, pull it free of the restraining right armpit and whip the free end clockwise around the

FIG. 155   **FIG. 156**   **FIG. 157**

body to strike the target from the left side. In this, as in the Release Pass, the idea is to change hands without letting the enemy see the action—hence the term, *Hsiao Kun,* "to vanish the rod."

RELEASE PASS

FIG. 155—Begin by swinging the nunchaku downward along the right side of the body past the knee, and then back up to wrap over the right shoulder, supposedly in preparation for striking down with an overhead blow to the enemy. Instead, trap the sakon under the right arm by clamping down with the right elbow. This is the most difficult part of the technique, and some hours of practice will be required to successfully catch the free rod as it swings over the shoulder. Note that, again, the left hand is held in front of the body defensively.

FIG. 156—From the previous position, pull down slightly with the right hand, creating a small amount of tension between the rods, then release your grip with the right hand and allow the sakon to drop behind the shoulder. Simultaneously, swing the left hand behind the back and catch the free end before it strikes the right hip.

This is known as *Shih Fang Kou,* or Release Pass.

FIG. 157—Gripping the sakon in the left hand, whip the ukon down behind the legs and out past the left side of the body. This swings the free end upward to strike the enemy from below.

FIG. 158

SHUANG CHIN KUN

As was stated at the outset, reliance on special devices to break in or escape can be easily overdone. This leads to dependence on those devices and a sense of loss when they are taken away. Neither of these alternatives is advisable.

Still, familiarity with such tools of the trade is a prerequisite for those who would pit themselves against the forces of the enemy. Further, exercise with the Shuang Chin Kun is excellent for developing hand-and-eye coordination and, in a pinch, their devastating effect can be a valuable asset (**FIG. 158**).

FIG. 159   FIG. 160

APPLICATION OF THE CAST

Having penetrated the enemy camp, advance to a position behind the sentry (Ashigaru) by employing the appropriate step from the Kuji Ashi.

FIG. 159—Load the nunchaku in casting position beside the right ear. Note that it is not necessary to approach the sentry as closely when armed as when unarmed, since the weapon extends the reach. Fix your attention on the base of the enemy skull.

FIG. 160—Cast the nunchaku as previously described, striking the enemy squarely on the base of the skull. If properly executed this attack will crush the back of the head and rupture the medulla oblongata, which controls the autonomic functions of the body, causing almost instant death. The enemy will not be able to cry out.

It should be noted that when attacking the enemy in this manner with the hand, a *shuto* (knife-hand chop) should be directed against the cervical vertebrae instead of the base of the skull. Such a blow would separate the bones of the neck, shearing the spinal column.

STRANGLING WITH SHUANG CHIN KUN

An auxiliary application of the Shuang Chin Kun is as a garrote. By looping the sageo (cord) over an extended limb or the enemy's neck and levering both rods together, an incredible amount of crushing pressure can be exerted.

FIG. 161　　　　　　　　**FIG. 162**

FIG. 161—Advance to a position behind the enemy. Hold the rods in the basic on-guard position—one in each hand, at chest level, with the cord taut. Approach to within arm's length of the enemy and fix the attention on the base of the skull.

FIG. 162—Step forward quickly and drop the cord over the enemy's head. Pull back strongly, snatching the cord into the enemy's larynx. This will prevent any outcry. Bring the hands together behind the enemy's head, crushing both sides of the enemy's neck between the rods. Retain your grip about the enemy's neck and drag him away backward to a place of concealment.

When this attack is properly executed, blood will spurt from the enemy ears as the muscles of the neck and the carotid sheath are crushed.

BLOCKING METHOD

Do not be limited in your application of the nunchaku when engaging the enemy, thinking only of strikes and methods of changing hands; rather, explore the other uses of the device.

An example of this is the use of both rods to deflect or forestall the enemy attack. Should the enemy discover your presence, turn, and draw his weapon to attack, allow him to thrust toward your solar plexus. (Should he attempt to cut, or slash, you will have to give ground and stay out of range.)

FIG. 163—As the point approaches, shift into a right sitting Horse Stance. This will allow the thrust to pass the body, while taking you out of the line of engagement. Strike sharply down with both rods held in one hand and beat the blade away from the front of the body.

FIG. 164—Immediately as the thrust is deflected, strike out strongly with the right back-fist action, hitting the enemy on his right temple. Keep the left hand in front of the body in a defensive position.

This attack will crush the temple, causing the enemy to drop like a felled ox. Even a light blow to this target will produce unconsciousness. This technique is derived from the art of *Tessenjitsu* (The Way of the Iron Fan), and is known as "fouling the blade."

MASS ATTACK

Should your presence be discovered and the enemy encircle your position, consider first the strategic aspects.

FIG. 165—Try to gain an advantage by getting your back to the wall. Keep the door on your right. Assume a stance of readiness, with the weapon drawn. Analyze the opponents and their positions. From left to right: A (in front of the door) blocks the escape, but can only

FIG. 163

FIG. 164

FIG. 165

attack the right side; B (left of center) will be the second to attack, following the most aggressive attacker by virtue of his more distant position; C (right of center) leads the attack; D (far right) must wait to attack lest he interfere with C's action.

Under ordinary circumstances, when confronted with multiple adversaries, it is advisable to attack the most aggressive first. Remember that he who fires first has a half-second edge, and the others will be slowed by the apparent lack of fear. Since the goal is escape, you must stall the enemy advance. Note in **FIG. 165** the eyes are directed toward opponent C. Opponent A, though, is nearest the weapon, and it is *he* who blocks the door.

FIG. 166—Swing out toward opponent C, whipping the sakon in front of him at eye level. This will break his momentum. Continue the whip past opponent B, even though he is still out of range. Strike opponent A strongly at solar plexus level; since his guard was high in the preceding figure, he is vulnerable to this attack.

FIG. 167—Immediately swing the sakon in a right hooking motion back past opponent B, who is still out of range, and strike opponent C on the right temple. This is possible since he was only made to hesitate in his initial attack and is still in range. Remember, aim to strike specific targets with the nunchaku. It is only an extension of the hand and arm, and strategic consideration should be the primary factor.

FIG. 166

FIG. 167

FIG. 168

Circle the sakon in front of the body in a clockwise direction, allowing the free end to swing above the head.

FIG. 168—Extend the arc and shift the body toward opponent B, who will now advance as the new standard-bearer seeing that the group's advance has been stopped. It is necessary to eliminate the most aggressive opponent as swiftly as possible, since he is most likely to continue the attack whether or not he interferes with his comrades' efforts.

Having rendered opponent B unconscious by striking the top of his head, now direct your attention to opponent D. He is the most dangerous. From the first, he selected a position farthest from the weapon, with his back covered. He waited for the first attack and gauged its effect. Now the weapon is away from him and the left side of the Ninja is open. He attacks by reaching in, seeking to get inside the arc of the weapon and attack the arm.

FIG. 169—Drop to the right knee and whip the sakon in a horizontal arc to attack the enemy low line by striking the knee.

The leading leg of the enemy is always a legitimate target, since it usually is the most extended part of his stance. And while this is a crippling attack, it does not prevent outcry. Any attack to the low line, be it knee, groin, or Hara, will cause the enemy to dip forward from the waist. This opens the back of the neck to an attack from above.

FIG. 170—Quickly turn to the left rear, rise, and assume a modified Twist Stance with the shoulders facing the enemy. Strike the target with a direct overhand chopping action, breaking the neck.

FIG. 169

FIG. 170

FIG. 171

FIG. 171—Return to your original stance, back to the wall, with the weight over the rear leg. Catch the sakon in the left hand and assume the basic on-guard position.

Remember, when facing multiple adversaries:

Position yourself so that only one can attack at a time. If two or more attack simultaneously, they will most often get in each other's way.

Keep the door on your right. This is advice from Miyamoto Musashi, who fought over two hundred duels and died of old age; it is not likely he was wrong.

Try to get your back to the wall. This limits the angles from which the enemy may attack.

Attack the most aggressive opponent first unless the exit is blocked, then clear the door first. It is always better to run than to face more than one opponent.

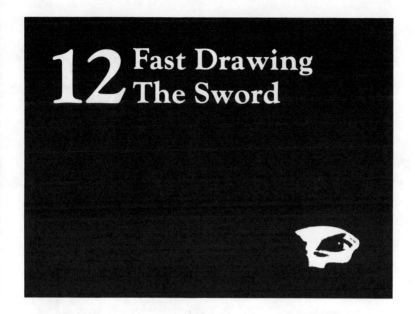

12 Fast Drawing The Sword

Iaijitsu, the Art of Fast Drawing the Sword, was an integral part of Ninja training. As the Sunday Punch of swordsmanship, it was often considered unethical. Nevertheless, it follows that the sword which finds its target first will be the victor.

The object of the quick draw is to cut the enemy down with a single stroke. Economy of movement is essential, as is accuracy.

SKY-TO-GROUND CUT

If the sword is worn on the left side with the edge down (as opposed to the Samurai katana), seize the moment of attack and advance on the enemy by stepping quickly forward with the left foot.

FIG. 172—Grasp the sword near the tsubo with the right hand, holding the scabbard with the left hand. Kiai or stamp your foot to make the enemy flinch and to disorient him.

When closing the distance between you and the enemy, bear in mind that he will most likely seek to fall back into his stance. Therefore, when attacking the body, advance one-half step; when attacking the head, advance one full step. In any event, your attack must be so sudden that no counterattack is possible.

FIG. 173—Swing the sword in an arc counterclockwise over the head, striking down on the enemy from above before his guard can be raised. This attack may be employed against the top of the head or, as shown here, to slash the subclavian artery which lies behind the collar-

127

FIG. 172   FIG. 173

bone. At longer range, one can strike off the hands or cut the forearms, then cut horizontally across the biceps or throat.

The attack must be so devastating that no recovery can be made.

GROUND-TO-SKY DRAW

Logically, this technique is the reverse of the preceding one. The former was a method of moving toward the enemy, an advance, while this method is employed at the instant the enemy attacks and is therefore a form of retreat.

FIG. 174—As the enemy launches his assault, step quickly back with the right foot, widening the distance between you and moving away from him. Grip the hilt with the left hand, holding the scabbard with the right behind the back. Again, the sword is worn edge down.

FIG. 175—Before the attack can reach you, whip the sword from the scabbard, turning the edge upward and striking him in the groin. This attack also can be used to sever the femoral artery along the inside of the thigh.

Note that the weight is shifted forward after the initial retreat to provide sufficient penetration of the enemy sphere. This attack is one

FIG. 174   FIG. 175

single, continuous, flowing, snapping action. Bear in mind that there is almost a full second of reaction time between an attack to the groin and the inevitable shock reaction. Some ryu train their members to utilize this second to effect a suicidal counterattack. Move after striking. This technique takes its name from the upward action of the blade.

HORIZONTAL DRAW

In many ways this method is the fastest of those shown, since it may be implemented with or without the illustrated side step. It is best to wait until the enemy begins his attack, since this will almost certainly cause him to raise his arms. Your attack can be made first, with kiai, if your aim is to attack his arm. Likewise, this attack is the one which is most often parried.

FIG. 176—As the enemy shifts his weight forward, seize the hilt in the right hand, the scabbard in the left, and draw the blade with the edge toward the outside line. This will entail twisting the scabbard with the left hand. The blade must be drawn horizontally for the cut to be at all effective.

FIG. 177—As the blade clears the scabbard, step to the side with the left foot, evading the enemy's intended attack, and grip the hilt

FIG. 176   FIG. 177

with the left hand below the right. Swing the sword as you would a baseball bat, slashing into the enemy rib cage and abdomen.

Normally the blade will stop when it reaches the spine. With a sword of sufficient caliber, the enemy can be cut in half by this technique.

SPINNING SWORD DRAW

This could be considered the horizontal draw with the left hand. Once again the target area is the rib cage and abdomen. Timing is critical, since you are actually moving toward the enemy as he advances toward you.

FIG. 178—The enemy launches his attack, in this case advancing to seize you with arms lifted. Grip the hilt with the left hand about halfway down from the tsubo, the scabbard, with the right hand behind the back, and draw the blade, edge down. Lower the center of gravity and bend the knees slightly.

FIG. 179—Cross the enemy path by stepping diagonally forward with your right foot. Drop to the right knee as you pass beneath his attack and spin toward your left rear corner. As your right foot touches

FIG. 178

FIG. 179

the ground, your right hand should grasp the sword hilt near the tsubo. Whip the blade in a horizontal arc as you spin, striking the enemy with a slashing stop-hit in midstride.

The technique may be completed by spinning the left leg toward the right forward corner, which places you behind the enemy, allowing you to make a vertical cut to the spine.

TARGET AREAS (FIG. 180)

Top of the Head—This target is generally attacked by the direct overhead cut.

Temple—The reverse or direct horizontal cut is employed when attacking the temple in an effort to ride over the guard.

Cheek—This secondary target is assaulted usually by the back cut or inner gate cut.

Throat—The straight thrust is the most effective attack to this quarter.

Forearm—This secondary target is attacked generally as a beat prior to the real attack.

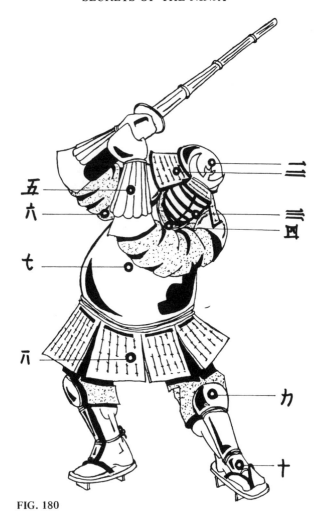

FIG. 180

Armpit—The most effective cut for this plexus is a sweeping upper-cut type of action. This is primarily a target of opportunity.

Solar Plexus—Again, the straight thrust is the most successful type of assault.

Groin—The uppercut attack, generally launched on the draw, is recommended.

Kneecap—Attacked by the low horizontal cut, this is primarily a secondary or beat target.

Instep—Attacked as a beat, or as a crippling blow, with the vertical cut from above.

13 The Nine Ways Of Throwing

One of the Ninja's most exotic arts is that of the *Tonki,* or small throwing weapons. These include the shuriken, throwing knives and axes, darts, eggshells filled with pepper and ashes, small grenades, caltrops, and coins.

Different ryu stressed different weapons, but all taught a variety of throwing techniques. These are detailed in the *Tonki-no-Kata,* or Nine Ways of Throwing, illustrated here with the shuriken **(FIG. 181)**.

CLASSICAL AX THROWING POSE

The most basic of all throwing methods is the Ax Throw, used by man over the centuries to cast his spear, hurl his battle-ax, or throw his dagger. It is a powerful throw which can be mastered in a few hours.

FIG. 182—Conceal the shuriken behind the shoulder. Draw the shuriken and grip it between the ball of the thumb and the first joint of the index finger; this position is known as the *knife-blade grip.* The weapon is now loaded beside the right ear. Extend the left arm to aim at the intended target.

(Note: This is the only movement in which one hand is free. In all of the others, as one weapon is launched, the next is being stolen in preparation for the next throw. This enables the Ninja to throw a variety of weapons in rapid-fire succession.)

AX THROW/WAIST STEAL

Throw the first shuriken by whipping the arm forward, snapping the wrist on the release to spin the weapon. This makes it fly more

FIG. 181   **FIG. 182**

accurately. The target area is the upper range of the enemy—the temple, eye, and side of the neck. The shuriken spins clockwise and flies vertically by this method.

FIG. 183—Simultaneously, the left arm falls back, *stealing* (a magician's term meaning "to pick up an object to be produced from its point of concealment without being observed") the second shuriken in preparation for the Waist Throw.

WAIST THROW/HIP STEAL

Cast the second shuriken by gripping it between the edges of the middle and ring fingers. This is known as the Coin Throw grip. It may take a little practice to master, but this method allows the shuriken to fly horizontally toward the central range of the enemy. When weapons are thrown from the waist using the knife-blade grip, they tend to wobble and lose accuracy. The target areas are the throat, solar plexus, and the pit of the stomach.

FIG. 184—As the second shuriken is thrown by the left hand, the right steals the third shuriken from the near hip (this may be the hip pocket or a small bag secured to the belt). This is the preparation for the Underhand Throw.

FIG. 183 **FIG. 184**

UNDERHAND THROW/COLLAR STEAL

Whip arm upward, straightening the elbow as the throw is made and again snapping the wrist. The target area is the low line of the enemy—the groin, femoral artery (inside the thigh), or knee. The shuriken flies vertically and the palm ends facing down.

FIG. 185—Simultaneously, the left hand steals the fourth shuriken from its place of concealment behind the collar. The Coin Throw grip is used to throw underhand and to grip the fourth weapon.

COIN THROW/ELBOW STEAL

From its position behind the left ear, snap the left forearm forward keeping the elbow bent. Check the forward motion of the left arm by jerking the right arm back from its Underhand Throw extension. Allow the left wrist to break forward as this contact is made. The shuriken is thus whipped over a short arc, flying straight to the target. This throw is most often used for throwing coins (filed down on one side to form an edge). It is highly prized by Kung Fu practitioners since the motion is small and easily concealable.

FIG. 185   **FIG. 186**

FIG. 186—As the Coin Throw is executed, the right hand steals the fifth shuriken from the forearm. The pocket may be on the inside or the outside of the arm, depending on personal preference.

BEHIND-THE-BACK THROW/CROSS-SHOULDER STEAL

From the previous position, throw straight back past the right hip using the knife-blade grip. This, of course, is directed at an enemy to the rear, and since most of the Tonki arsenal was employed to slow down enemy pursuit, it was one of the most practiced. The palm ends facing up.

FIG. 187—The left hand steals the sixth shuriken from the front of the shoulder during the Behind-the-Back Throw. The place of concealment could be either the breast pocket or the strap of a combat harness. The knife-blade grip is employed for this steal.

BETWEEN-THE-LEGS THROW/ANKLE STEAL

Twist the hips so that another attack from the rear is simulated. Snap the shuriken downward, striking the inside of the leg to check the

FIG. 187   **FIG. 188**

action of the arm, and whip the shuriken behind you in a manner similar to the Coin Throw action. In this throw, the weapon is not directed straight toward the target, but rather is inclined upward. Thus the action is from low to high range, with the shuriken flying vertically.

   FIG. 188—Simultaneously, the right hand steals the seventh shuriken from the ankle bag or calf scabbard. The knife-blade grip is used for the next throw.

SIDEARM THROW/NEAR LAPEL STEAL

   From the previous crouched position, raise the body and turn into the enemy, slinging the shuriken horizontally much as a baseball pitcher winds up and throws. Like the Ax Throw, this is a strong technique. It is usually directed against the central target area. This method and the previous two throws (Behind-the-Back and Between-the-Legs) were the primary techniques taught by all ryu. A Ninja fleeing for his life could throw straight behind without stopping, or stop suddenly in a wide stance and throw, or turn suddenly to throw in defense.

FIG. 189　　　　　　　　　　FIG. 190

FIG. 189—As the right hand throws, the left steals the next shuriken from the near side lapel using the knife-throw grip. This is the opposite of the Cross-Shoulder Steal.

DART THROW/BELT BUCKLE STEAL

The Dart Throw differs from the other techniques shown in that no spin is given to the weapon. This is a short-range technique used to launch a missile point-first toward the target. The action is a short stroking motion with the arm continuing to arc downward after the dart is released.

FIG. 190—The right hand steals the ninth shuriken from behind the center of the belt (behind the buckle). In this action, the weapon is not gripped, but rather cupped in the palm. This method is the preparation for the Sand Toss, or may be used to throw a handful of caltrops or similar missiles.

SAND TOSS THROW/OVER-SHOULDER STEAL

The ninth shuriken is thrown up from the waist *between* the Ninja and the enemy. The idea is to temporarily blind the enemy or make

FIG. 191

him flinch, allowing time to escape. The palm is facing upward at the conclusion of this technique.

FIG. 191—At this point the entire sequence is repeated, beginning with the Ax Throw on the left side. From the position shown, the right hand turns palm down and aims at the target, while the left arm reaches over the shoulder to draw the next weapon. By these means alone, it is possible to throw eighteen shurikens with machine-gun rapidity, each throw setting up the next. Few pursuers would be able to continue against such a barrage. And all that is required is that they stop for a moment, allowing the skillful Ninja to vanish.

14 Capture In Passing

Ninjitsu is known as the Art of Invisibility. Inpo, the Art of Hiding, teaches us how to remain unseen once we are out of the enemy's view. Tonpo, likewise, teaches us how to vanish from the view of the enemy. The techniques of *Huo Nei Kuo* are the basis for this ability.

Translated to mean "capture in passing," the term is related to the stratagem in chess of overcoming the enemy pawns should they fail to act. These techniques are the basis for many legends about masters of the martial arts who would overcome an opponent with no physical contact. In each case it is possible to evade the enemy's attack without killing him. For this reason the *Mi Lu Kata* from which the techniques are drawn is sometimes known as the Way of Fighting Without Fighting.

KASUMI (CLOUDING THE MIND)

This method is employed when the enemy is poised in a wide stance, but has not yet advanced. Lower the body slightly for better balance. Relax both wrists so the hands hang loosely with the backs to the enemy. Assume a Horse Stance. This will sometimes induce the enemy to widen his stance since he will expect lateral movement from you. You should be three to five feet from the enemy. Raise the hands, arms extended between you, aiming the back of the wrists at the enemy face. You must do this not so slowly that he reacts before you are ready, and not so quickly that he will ignore the movement. Watch your own hands—this will induce the enemy to do likewise. The idea is to focus his attention on your hands.

FIG. 192   FIG. 193

FIG. 192—Step quickly forward, lowering the body still more. This will move the hands toward the enemy but, since the arms are not moving and the perspective is foreshortened, you will be upon him before he can react. As the right foot touches the ground, flick the fingers into the face of the enemy. Regardless of whether you actually touch his face or merely flash him, he will flinch or blink. This is an autonomic reflex and is virtually uncontrollable.

Immediately as you flash or haze the enemy, drop straight down over the feet into a squatting position. You will not see the enemy blink, since you are looking over the ends of your wrists and, by lifting the fingers, you will obscure his face from view. The haze will cause the enemy to raise his guard to protect his eyes. Since you will be crouched almost at his knee level, you will be screened from view by his own arms.

FIG. 193—As you sink out of sight, and see the enemy lifting his guard, tuck your head into your chest, round the shoulders, and push off with both feet. The momentum of this effort will carry you between the enemy's legs. Execute a forward roll as your hands touch the ground behind him. This will enable you to vanish downward to a position ten feet behind the enemy.

T'IAO UKE (VAULTING THE ENEMY)

This method is employed when the enemy attempts a low-line attack, such as a leg dive or tackle.

FIG. 194—The enemy steps forward, dropping his shoulders and reaching in to seize the knees. Effect a back-out step by slapping down onto his back with both hands and kicking both feet straight to the rear. This prevents the leg dive and stalls the enemy in a forward leaning stance.

FIG. 195—Push off with both hands and jump straight up spreading the legs. The combination of the enemy's forward momentum and your own spring will carry him under you. Some practitioners prefer to grip the enemy head when vaulting, thus insuring that it remain low enough to prevent accidental groin injuries.

Any type of Roman Horse vault will suffice to clear the enemy, depending on the acrobatic agility of the practitioner and the depth at which the enemy attacks. In this way, one vanishes upward to a position three to five feet behind the enemy.

FIG. 194

FIG. 195

HSING TSIA (GO BEHIND STEP)

This method requires an external distraction to be truly effective. Two methods are preferred, one being kiai, the spirit shout. Sometimes called the "attack by intimidation," the kiai is a belly shout drawn from the Hara. It is a scream of total commitment. Charge the enemy from out of range, feinting a ferocious attack to the eyes. This attack must be sufficiently terrifying to startle the enemy and make him cover his own eyes in defense. The kiai may be employed effectively with the Kasumi technique.

Sha Nei Mu, or "sand in the eyes," is the second distraction which is used to temporarily blind the enemy. Some schools devise complex fomulas for their blinding powders. Itching and sneezing dust are two obvious examples. In ancient times these were stored in hollowed-out eggshells, so they could be brought quickly into play. A handful of native dirt will produce the same effect if one can be surreptitiously obtained.

FIG. 196—Cup the right palm lightly, keeping the dust concealed from the enemy. Swing the arm in a semicircular arc, crossing from the right to left hip, up to the left shoulder, then back in front of the right shoulder. Abruptly stop the right palm in an extended shoulder-block position, casting the powder into the face of the enemy. As you begin the casting movement, step toward the left. This will give the impression that you are attempting to flee in that direction and distract the enemy's attention from the action of the right arm.

FIG. 197—As the enemy gropes forward toward what he believes to be your position, duck under his attack to his lead side. In this way you will have less distance to travel to get behind him. This is an extended variation of the Spinning Back Pivot found in Inpo. Fix your attention on the left temple of the enemy. This is where you will strike him should he somehow not have been blinded.

If you are close enough to the enemy, the action of casting will carry your extended finger tips horizontally across the enemy's eyes,

FIG. 196

FIG. 197   FIG. 198

producing the desired effect. This attack is also found in Wing Chun, but is followed by a palm-up finger jab.

FIG. 198—Execute the second half of the Mi Lu pivot, slipping by the enemy as his grasp closes on emptiness. You are now invisible behind his own left shoulder. Continue to target his left temple.

You may now pivot into the final Mi Lu position and assume a stance behind the enemy, or dart behind cover to vanish, or simply flee (FIG. 199).

In this way, you vanish completely—in full view of the enemy.

FIG. 199

15 Leaving No Trace

In Ninjitsu, it is essential that little evidence of the methods used remains for the enemy to study. Thus, we strive to leave no trace of our passing for the enemy to follow.

When being pursued, and the enemy cannot be outrun, the options are few. The Ninja can stand and fight, in which event the foremost enemy should be killed as savagely as possible, striking terror into the hearts of his fellows. Or, he can shake off the enemy by means of false trails carrying the pursuit away from his actual position.

One method of shaking off the enemy is known as the *false exit*. Gaining sufficient lead from the enemy to escape his view, open a door or gate and leave it ajar as you pass. Few people will leave an outside door open, and virtually no security installation would tolerate it. The enemy in hot pursuit would be faced with the decision of which path to take. At the least, this should induce him to divide his forces.

A similar technique is known as *disturbing the dust*. It calls for leaving footprints in an area where they can be seen by the enemy. Running by means of the Heng Pu leaves tracks which seem to travel in both directions at once. *Back-tracking* is a variation of this. It involves allowing the enemy to overrun your concealed position as he follows a previously prepared trail, then doubling back to your real intent.

Chia Ying, or the false shadow, is a technique for using an S-shaped candle to hide the Ninja's position. In ancient times, such a candle could be hung on projecting cornices or brush, giving the impression that the assassin was standing holding a candle where there were no places to set one. Modern police officers utilize a similar technique in holding their flashlights away from the body. A suspect would naturally assume the light to be in front of the body and fire at that.

Ametori no jitsu is probably the most famous method of concealing the true escape route. It is based on the principle that a raincoat always implies the presence of the person inside. Thus, a cloak or suit of armor could be positioned so that it appeared to be a person standing, producing the same effect as a scarecrow.

Whenever possible it is advisable to create confusion in the enemy. Overlook nothing. Utilize meteorological phenomena such as rain, a sudden flash of lightning, the passing of the moon behind a cloud, blinding sunlight, and deceptive moonlight. All should be considered.

Fire is an excellent diversion which will create confusion. Fire at strategic sites in the camp is best used to cover escape rather than entry, since it will arouse the enemy and put him on guard. Fire on the perimeter can be used to drive the enemy back.

Lastly, consider *terminating the trail*. The ancient Ninja were masters of this. Lead the enemy to a precipice and disappear, leaving no trace; lead the enemy into a trap; or lead the enemy to an intersection leaving no clue as to which path was taken. In short, escape his pursuit in such a manner that he will believe you have vanished into thin air. To accomplish this, one must be a master of Inpo.

16 The Mission

For here you are,
A cogless, meshless, automaton;
A body upon whom officials had performed clinical autopsy,
And left all of you that mattered back upon empty seas,
And strewn over darkened hills.

Here you are,
Bone dry, bottle empty, fireless.
Chill, with only your hands to give death to men.
A pair of hands is all you are now . . .

(Ashida Kim)

Erich Fromm, the noted psychologist, once said that "the function of any ethical system in any given society is to sustain the life of that society." He neglected to mention that any system can consider itself ethical. Thus it falls to the Ninja to determine which mission he will undertake.

Missions are divided into three major categories:

Sabotage includes disrupting the enemy camp as well as eliminating strategic points along the enemy perimeter which will allow an assault to succeed.

Espionage deals with the gathering of intelligence about the enemy. This may be done surreptitiously, or data gathered by the enemy may be boldly stolen.

Assassination is an art unto itself. It may take the form of poisons, booby traps, or murder. Needless to say, the ability to get in and out without being discovered is a prerequisite.

A Ninja will not sacrifice himself; he will not be swayed by emotional appeals; and he does not question the motives of those who would employ him. Should he accept their commission, he will become their hands, and accomplish that which they could not.

Ninjitsu is a way of doing anything or nothing—simply being. Invisibility is merely the focus of the art.

MUGEI-MUMEI-NO-JITSU (NO NAME, NO ART)

Ninjitsu as revealed herein is essentially a pragmatic art. It will employ any technique from any source which will serve its purpose. It strives always to be one with the natural order of things. This is the true meaning of passing without leaving a trace.

It is said that the Ninja can walk through walls; that when they are looked for, they cannot be seen; when listened for, they cannot be heard; and when they are felt for, they cannot be touched. A Ninja never swaggers—his gait is firm and straight ahead. He neither makes a show of force, nor beats his own drum. This is known as *Mugei-Mumei-no-Jitsu*, "no name, no art."

A Ninja does not surrender peaceably, nor does he carry on his person documents which might implicate his superiors. The Ninja acts alone, relying on his own ability. He is one with himself.

What will happen in one's life is already written, but one must choose to be there. This is the Way of Ninjitsu.

*The way that
can be told is not
the eternal way . . .
it cannot
be explained
or defined,
it can only
be experienced.*